TOPICS **TODAY**

T0002964

Feminism and Gender Equality

By Michelle Denton

Cavendish Square

New York

Published in 2021 by Cavendish Square Publishing, LLC
243 5th Avenue, Suite 136, New York, NY 10016

First Edition

Website: cavendishsq.com

This publication represents the opinions and views of the author based on his or her personal experience, knowledge, and research. The information in this book serves as a general guide only. The author and publisher have used their best efforts in preparing this book and disclaim liability rising directly or indirectly from the use and application of this book.

All websites were available and accurate when this book was sent to press.

Library of Congress Cataloging-in-Publication Data

Names: Denton, Michelle, author.
Title: Feminism and gender equality / Michelle Denton.
Description: First Edition. | New York : Cavendish Square Publishing, 2021.
| Series: Topics today | Includes bibliographical references and index.
Identifiers: LCCN 2020007779 (print) | LCCN 2020007780 (ebook) | ISBN 9781502657459 (library binding) | ISBN 9781502657442 (paperback) | ISBN 9781502657466 (ebook)
Subjects: LCSH: Feminism–Juvenile literature. | Women's rights–Juvenile literature.
Classification: LCC HQ1155 .D476 2021 (print) | LCC HQ1155 (ebook) | DDC 305.42–dc23
LC record available at https://lccn.loc.gov/2020007779
LC ebook record available at https://lccn.loc.gov/2020007780

Editor: Jennifer Lombardo
Copy Editor: Michelle Denton
Designer: Deanna Paternostro

Some of the images in this book illustrate individuals who are models. The depictions do not imply actual situations or events.

CPSIA compliance information: Batch #CS20CSQ: For further information contact Cavendish Square Publishing LLC, New York, New York, at 1-877-980-4450.

Printed in China

Find us on

No nation can rise above the level of its womanhood

WHAT IS FEMINISM?

Women's rights have been a major topic of discussion for a long time, and since 2010, the conversation has become even more intense. As issues such as sexual harassment and reproductive rights become increasingly highlighted in the media, more people are beginning to tackle important questions about gender in their daily lives. Why do we treat women and men differently? Does nature or society influence gender more? What makes something or someone feminine or masculine, and what does it mean to be in-between? The growth and spread of these ideas are due to a social movement called feminism.

The dictionary definition of feminism is "the theory of the political, economic, and social equality of the sexes."[1] This means that feminists want everyone to have the same access to opportunities and human rights. This concept is also known as gender equality. Feminists focus on gender—and particularly women—because they believe most cultures have oppressed women as well as transgender and nonbinary people by taking away their rights and opportunities throughout most of history.

The word "feminism" was first used in the mid-1800s by French philosopher Charles Fourier, at a time when women in Europe and North America were beginning to fight for their rights. In these places and other areas influenced by European,

◀ From the mid-1800s into the early 20th century, suffragettes, such as those shown here, were instrumental in helping women win the right to vote.

or Western, culture, gender equality was practically unheard of at the time. Since ancient times, Western culture had been a patriarchy, or a society ruled by men. When people say "the patriarchy," they're generally talking about the patriarchy that dominates Western society.

What Is a Patriarchy?

A patriarchy is a system of social organization where males hold the primary positions of power in society. Western culture is a patriarchy. Feminists argue that the Western patriarchy gives men—specifically cisgender men, meaning those whose gender identity matches their assigned sex—a disproportionate amount of power over women and people of other genders. In order to maintain this kind of culture, cisgender women, transgender people, and nonbinary people must have their power taken away by limiting their rights, such as the right to vote or the right to privacy, and their opportunities, such as what careers they can have or who they can marry.

Trying to force gender roles on children sets up a pattern of social behavior that limits their choices and expectations. This can negatively affect both boys and girls.

Although many arguments focus on the patriarchy's effects on women, it hurts men too. The strict gender roles forced upon men, such as being expected to be dominant and unemotional, have led to mental health issues, domestic abuse, and high rates of suicide around the world. Under the patriarchy, many young boys are told that "crying is for girls" or are shamed for "throwing like a girl," and the negative emotions attached to those situations create strict forms of behavior; both men and women who conform to the patriarchy tend to believe that a "real" man is strong, dominant, and hides his feelings, while a "real" woman is weak, delicate, and has difficulty controlling herself. These feminine traits are seen as naturally, or inherently, inferior and—at the same time—desirable or even required in women. This harmful mindset teaches both men and women that because women are feminine and feminine traits are bad, men are inherently better than women.

Sexism and Misogyny

Sexism is prejudice, or nonfactual negative beliefs, and discrimination against someone because of their gender, and in most cases it refers to prejudice and discrimination against women. It's sexist when people say women as a whole are less intelligent or less funny than men, or when a woman is passed over for a promotion simply because she's a woman. Feminists would say that the patriarchy is inherently sexist because it requires prejudice against women to maintain a male-dominated power structure.

From the Greek roots *misein*, "to hate," and *gyne*, "woman," misogyny is the hatred of women. Some men are so prejudiced against women that it leads them to be dismissive, angry, or violent when their views are challenged. "I define misogyny as social systems or environments where women face hostility and hatred because they're women in a man's world—a historical patriarchy,"[2] said Cornell philosophy professor Kate Manne in an interview. Misogyny can involve physical, verbal, emotional, or sexual violence. It's misogynistic when someone harasses a woman online because she expressed her opinion or when a man beats his wife.

Although both are methods of controlling the power balance under the patriarchy, experts believe it's important to know the difference between sexism and misogyny. Manne went on to say that "sexism is the ideology that *supports* patriarchal social relations, but misogyny *enforces* it when there's a threat of that system going away."[3] In other words, sexism is generally a passive way of maintaining the patriarchy, while misogyny is active.

Are We All Equal?

Some people say there's no need for feminism in the modern world. Because of the huge strides in women's rights that have been made

Although there have been great strides toward equality, the progress that has been made is constantly under attack, even today. Many feminists have spoken out against laws that limit the reproductive decisions a woman can make, such as using birth control.

since the 1800s, many believe that there are no more fights to be won. Women in Western culture can vote, go to school, and have careers; asking for more, in some people's opinion, is greedy and nit-picky. They believe that the problems feminists see in society aren't serious ones.

Feminists would say that despite the rights and opportunities women now have, there are still issues with how women, transgender (often shortened to trans) people, and nonbinary people are treated because of their gender. They make less money than men at the same jobs, and their reproductive rights are under constant threat of being taken away. Sexual assault and harassment are common. Women around the world are denied education, health care, and safety. LGBTQ+ people are made to suffer for being themselves. These and other problems make feminism, and a feminist future, very important.

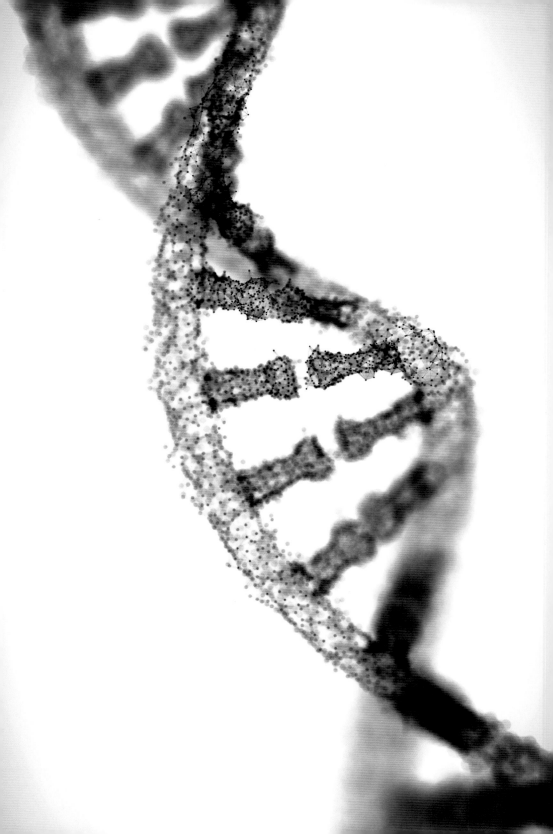

CHAPTER ONE

A SOCIAL CONSTRUCT

Gender is a social construct, meaning that it exists "as a result of human interaction. It exists because humans agree that it exists."[1] Humans made it up. It isn't part of objective reality and doesn't exist outside of human society. A simple example of a social construct is money: Humans give dollars and coins meaning, but in objective reality, they are simply pieces of paper and metal. The same is true of gender: Humans assign meaning to how a person looks and acts, but in objective reality, a person simply exists and those things have no greater meaning.

At the center of the gender equality issue are the constructs of sex and gender and what they mean. Does someone's biology influence their strengths and weaknesses in unchangeable ways, or are people products of their environment, with their strengths and weaknesses influenced by what they're encouraged to do? This nature versus nurture debate has been raging for a long time, but researchers suggest that human behavior is the result of a bit of both. Child psychiatrist David Rettew stated that

> most scientists ... have come to appreciate that the nature and nurture domains are hopelessly interwoven with one another. Genes have an influence on the environments we experience. At the same time, a person's environment and

◄ Although a person's DNA determines their probability of having certain traits, there are many variations when it comes to sex chromosomes, which makes determining someone's sex more complicated than it might seem.

experience can directly change the level at which certain genes are expressed … which in turn alters both the physical structure and activity of the brain.[2]

Our environment—our culture—has very strict guidelines when it comes to gender, and they influence people very strongly. From a feminist perspective, these guidelines are meant to uphold the patriarchy and are harmful when they limit what a person can do.

Sex and Genetics

Sex and gender are often confused as the same idea, but they're very different. Sex is biologically determined, but it isn't as simple as some believe. Human beings don't only come in the two categories of female and male. Instead, there are many sexes a person could be.

A person's deoxyribonucleic acid (DNA) determines the probability of them having certain traits. Chromosomes are the part of DNA that carry genetic material. People are generally born with 46 chromosomes in 23 pairs, one pair of which are sex chromosomes—X or Y. Most people who are assigned female at birth are 46XX, denoting how many chromosomes they have and what kind of sex chromosomes they have. Most people who are assigned male at birth are 46XY. According to the World Health Organization (WHO):

Research suggests, however, that in a few births per thousand some individuals will be born with a single sex chromosome (45X or 45Y) … and some with three or more sex chromosomes (47XXX, 47XYY or 47XXY, etc.) … In addition, some males are born 46XX due to the translocation [movement] of a tiny section of the sex determining region of the Y chromosome. Similarly, some females are also born 46XY due to mutations in the Y chromosome.[3]

People whose DNA is like this are known as intersex. These genetic variants can influence a person's hormones and sex organs, but not always; in some cases, there may be no way to tell if someone is intersex without a DNA test.

Humans like categories because they make the world easier to understand. However, they can also be harmful when they become strictly enforced. Although some cultures have historically acknowledged intersex people, many have not. Before and during the development of modern medical science, people categorized those with vaginas as female and those with penises as male, and anyone else was believed to have a medical problem. Today, doctors and scientists know that being intersex is a natural occurrence and isn't something that needs to be fixed.

When a child is born, they're generally assigned either female or male based on what their sex organs look like, but this is only a guess at both the child's sex and gender. Alice Dreger, a historian of science and medicine, said, "We now know that sex is complicated enough that we have to admit nature doesn't draw the line for us between male and female ... we actually draw that line on nature."[4]

What scientists do know is that biology can influence who someone is; for example, someone who doesn't have a strong gene for muscle tone may find it difficult to become an athlete. However, that doesn't mean they could never become an athlete; they could train hard and overcome their genetic limitations. Also, there's no evidence to support the idea that genes discriminate based on sex. In other words, science hasn't proven that all men are genetically strong or that all women are genetically more emotionally expressive.

Assigning Gender

Assigned sex is typically translated into assigned gender. A person born with a vagina is assigned female and assumed to be a girl, and a person born with a penis is assigned male and assumed to be a boy. However, this a simplistic way of thinking about gender, and many people reject these categories in one way or another as they grow older.

WHO defines gender as "the socially constructed characteristics of women and men—such as norms, roles and relationships of and between groups of women and men. It varies from society to society and can be changed."[5] There are two components to gender: gender expression and gender identity.

Gender is expressed through repeated acts, and it is a complex balancing of what is expressed to the outside world and what is felt and believed within a person.

Many feminists believe gender is performative, meaning that people create their gender through the interaction between what they say and do and how society interprets what they say and do. American philosopher and gender theorist Judith Butler believed that gender "is not something one is, it is something one does; it is a sequence of acts, a doing rather than a being. And repeatedly engaging in 'feminising' and 'masculinising' acts congeals gender thereby making people falsely think of gender as something they naturally *are*. Gender only comes into being through these gendering acts."[6] This is gender expression—the external display of someone's gender. It can involve any form of self-expression, including hairstyle, makeup, clothes, and body modifications such as tattoos and piercings, as well as how someone moves, talks, and interacts with their environment.

How someone interprets their own words, actions, and thoughts is of equal, if not more, importance. This is gender identity, a person's internal sense of their gender. Sociologists believe that children develop their gender identity by the age of three. Generally, people match their gender expression to their gender identity so other people will interpret their gender correctly.

The Language of Sex and Gender

AFAB: assigned female at birth

AMAB: assigned male at birth

cisgender: a gender identity that corresponds with the sex a person was assigned at birth; sometimes shortened to cis

dysphoria: discomfort, such as confusion and depression, related to the difference between a person's gender identity and sex assigned at birth

gender nonconforming: having a gender expression that does not follow gender norms

intersex: a sex assigned when a person is born with a combination of female and male biological characteristics, such as genitals or chromosomes

nonbinary: a gender identity that is neither entirely female nor entirely male; refers to a spectrum of identities, including agender, bigender, genderfluid, and many others, as well as to a single gender identity

pronoun: a part of speech that replaces a proper noun such as a name, i.e. he/him, she/her, they/them, xe/xem, ze/zem, and others

sexual orientation: a person's sexual and emotional attraction to others that can combine characteristics such as gender expression and sex assigned at birth

transgender: a gender identity that differs from the sex a person was assigned at birth

Children and Gender Socialization

Gender socialization is a process that occurs during childhood and involves learning the social roles that are expected of someone's gender in their culture. It's typically based on a child's assigned sex and gender, but it doesn't necessarily correlate, or connect, with their gender identity. Parents or guardians, teachers, peers, and the media all play a part in gender socialization by enforcing and reinforcing gender roles.

Gender socialization begins even before birth. Assigning a sex to an unborn baby through ultrasound is very important to some families, and many people have gender reveal parties to celebrate and assign their child's gender. In many cases, knowing a baby's assigned sex and gender before they're born leads parents and family members to buy gendered items—pink for girls and blue for boys. Because of this, children are often introduced to gender stereotypes immediately after they're born because of the color of their clothes and toys.

As children grow up, they begin taking notice of gender roles and often change their behavior and attitudes accordingly. This knowledge comes from interacting with other people. First, they learn from their parents or guardians, siblings, and other family, then from other children their own age as they start socializing outside the home, and then from teachers when they enter school. In all of these situations, children are testing the boundaries of what's socially acceptable. For example, on a playground, a girl may be discouraged from getting dirty or running too fast, while a boy may be encouraged to climb or swing as high as he can. This tells the girl that she's expected to be less active than the boy, which may discourage her from pursuing sports, building things, or taking classes related to fast-paced, physically active careers. These same statements tell the boy that he is expected to be more active than the girl, which may discourage him from pursuing writing, art, or other slower-paced careers.

Many parts of our society maintain these expectations, including most media, such as movies, television, and books. Even everyday environments reinforce gender roles, or ways different genders are expected to look and act. Retail stores, for instance, often reinforce gender roles with the way they set up their children's clothing and toy sections. The sections might be right next to each other, but they're typically color coded: pinks and yellows for girls, blues and greens for boys. Although many parents allow their children to wear whatever color or "gender" of clothes they want, some expect their children to only wear clothes made for their assigned gender. Some have double standards, possibly without realizing it. For example,

Gendered clothing often reinforces gender roles, and it shapes and defines children as their assigned sex from birth, regardless of their actual gender identity.

a mother may allow her daughter to wear jeans and play with model cars but not allow her son to wear a dress and play with dolls. Lisa Dinella, a researcher at the Gender Development Laboratory, noted that all of this sends a message: "Kids notice the subtle cues that are part of the toys that leads them to decide that a toy is a girl toy or a boy toy, and whether it's for them or not for them. And it actually changes their interest in the toy and so that is guiding kids' play activities."[7]

Limiting Stereotypes

Although a toy's color may not seem like a big deal, gender socialization can limit what a person believes they can be and do. When a young girl is told not to climb as high as the boys, made fun of for being loud, or encouraged to play house instead of superheroes, she's learning that women are expected to be passive, quiet, and nurturing even if those things conflict with her personality. In the same way, when boys are encouraged to fight, told not to cry, and discouraged from playing with dolls, they are being taught that men are expected to be aggressive, unemotional, and removed from anything considered "feminine." Navigating gender socialization can be even harder for trans and nonbinary children, since they're often socialized as a gender they don't identify with. When the way someone is being raised conflicts with their gender identity, they often feel unhappy and may even develop dysphoria. Strict gender expectations ultimately harm people as they grow up and find that certain parts of themselves don't fit the stereotype.

The way our society is structured teaches people that women and men are fundamentally, unchangeably different, and many believe it and continue the cycle. This can affect people's daily lives more than they may realize. Women, transgender people, and

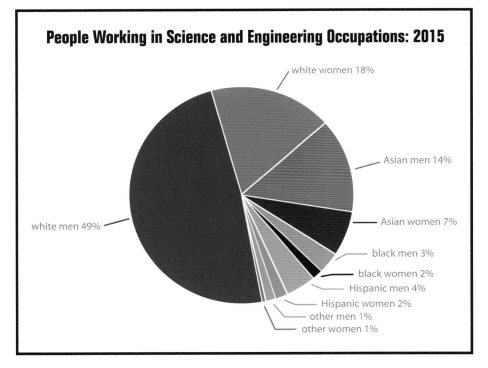

People Working in Science and Engineering Occupations: 2015

white women 18%

Asian men 14%

Asian women 7%

black men 3%

black women 2%

Hispanic men 4%

Hispanic women 2%

other men 1%

other women 1%

white men 49%

As this information from the National Science Foundation shows, men of every race outnumber women of their same race in science and engineering fields. White men outnumber all other segments of the population. This may partially be due to the fact that women are often discouraged from pursuing these kinds of careers.

nonbinary people are often forced to live their lives in constant conflict with the patriarchy. For example, women who pursue careers sometimes limit themselves because of what the patriarchy has told them about who they should be, even if they don't know they're limiting themselves. "They lack confidence in their ability to compete in fields that men are stereotypically believed to perform more strongly in, such as science, math, and technology," noted Dina Gerdeman, a writer for Harvard Business School. "Women are also more reluctant to share their ideas in group discussions on these subjects. And even when they have talent—and are actually told they are high-achievers in these subjects—women are more likely than men to shrug off the praise and lowball [underestimate] their own abilities."[8]

Stereotypes limit people's opportunities and can affect their ability to exercise their rights. If someone believes women are weak, they may not give a woman the opportunity to work on a construction site even if she's qualified for the job. If someone believes women are unintelligent, they may try to prevent women from voting.

Rejecting Gender Essentialism

Many people argue that our modern gender roles and stereotypes are part of the natural order of the world, passed down through history and our genes. Thinking this way is called gender essentialism, a concept that states that there are natural, unchangeable qualities to women and men. Many feminists reject essentialism, not only because it limits everyone but also because it's often used to discredit and exclude trans and nonbinary people for not fitting into these narrow categories. Anthropologists (researchers who study cultures), sociologists (researchers who study social behavior), and historians disagree that humans are naturally only one thing or another. They tend to believe that most human social traits, such as gender, are on a spectrum that changes throughout time as society changes.

In the past, cultures around the world developed in various different ways, and not all of them were or are strictly patriarchal. By studying modern hunter-gatherer tribes and our closest animal relatives, chimpanzees, anthropologists have concluded that gender equality was important in the development of early human society.

Although gender roles did exist in the form of labor division, these roles were likely not as strict or as oppressive toward women as many people today believe. Some societies, such as some Native American cultures, were matriarchies, where women controlled the majority of the political and social power. Many Native American cultures also recognized nonbinary genders that are collectively referred to as "two-spirit" today.

Some people lose sight of history and make arguments against feminist gender theory based on the idea that gender roles and stereotypes have always been the same and are therefore "just how it is." However, historians point out that many gender stereotypes, such as girls liking pink and boys liking blue, didn't exist even 100 years ago. In June 1918, the trade publication *Earnshaw's Infants' Department* published an article that read, "The generally accepted rule is pink for the boys, and blue for the girls. The reason is that pink, being a more decided and stronger color, is more suitable for the boy, while blue, which is more delicate and dainty, is prettier for the girl."[9] Even more commonly, young children were dressed in gender-neutral white. Putting girls exclusively in pink and putting boys exclusively in blue didn't arise until the 1940s, when clothing companies realized they were losing money because gender-neutral clothes could be passed down from one child to the next within a family. Gendering clothes was a marketing strategy to keep parents from recycling their son's baby clothes when they had a daughter.

Toxic Masculinity

In some cases, the enforcement of gender roles can make people toxic to themselves and those around them. Feminists are most concerned with toxic masculinity, which happens when "common masculine ideals such as social respect, physical strength, and sexual potency become problematic when they set unattainable standards. Falling short can make boys and men insecure and anxious, which might prompt them to use force in order to feel, and be seen as, dominant and in control."[10] Most often seen in cis men, toxic masculinity is generally seen as the root cause of issues such as sexual assault and domestic violence. "It's a manhood that views women and

Before the 1940s, it was common practice for babies and toddlers to wear unisex white dresses that could be passed down from one child to the next. This photo from 1909 shows Eleanor and Franklin Roosevelt with their son and daughter.

Unnecessarily Gendered Products

Walking down the grooming products aisle at the supermarket, it's common to see a striking difference between the products marketed to women and those marketed to men. Products for women tend to be white with pops of bright colors, while products for men tend to be black, gray, or dark brown. In most cases, these products are exactly the same except for the color of the product or packaging, but gender roles are so strictly enforced that many people accept this marketing strategy as a natural part of the world and not as the result of a company board meeting. Some people actually feel discomfort if they aren't able to use a product that's marketed directly to them; for instance, some men simply refuse to use women's razors, even if the only difference is that the razor is pink.

Occasionally, however, a product is so unnecessarily gendered that it makes major waves. A famous example of this phenomenon is the BIC For Her pens, which come in pink and purple and are marketed as soft and comfortable for women's hands. In response to their launch, people flooded the Amazon page for the pens with sarcastic, satirical reviews such as, "My husband got me these ladypens because I find manpens to be so taxing. Thank god he knows what a delicate flower I am,"[1] and, "So now they have their own pens. Next thing, they will be owning property, voting, and talking back. Where will it end?"[2]

In addition to the ridiculous nature of these marketing ploys, another issue with color-coded products is the "pink tax." Products such as razors, deodorants, soaps, and many others cost about 13 percent more when they're pink and marketed toward women, and products such as pads and tampons are highly taxed as "luxury" items, or things people don't truly need to buy, even though they are necessary for anyone who gets their period. Even clothing and toys cost more for women and girls, for no reason other than that companies believe they can get away with it. However, this moneymaking scheme reinforces the idea that men and women are different even when they're buying the same product in different colored boxes.

1. LakeviewFamily, "My Husband Got Me These Ladypens," Amazon review, January 9, 2018, www.amazon.com/review/R1YN1OS37BQMQZ.

2. PaulM, "Where Will It End?," Amazon review, May 9, 2013, www.amazon.com/review/R2A96OCYB4Z8HS.

LGBT people as inferior, sees sex as an act not of affection but domination, and which [validates] violence as the way to prove one's self to the world," wrote Salon politics writer Amanda Marcotte. "Toxic masculinity aspires to toughness but is, in fact, an ideology of living in fear: The fear of ever seeming soft, tender, weak, or somehow less than manly."[11]

This is not to say that all masculinity is toxic; many traditionally masculine traits can be positive. There is nothing wrong with being physically strong, seeking basic respect, being the breadwinner, or going after what you want. Contrary to popular opinion, most feminists don't think men or masculinity are evil. In fact, seeing men as inherently evil takes any responsibility for their actions away from them; it makes it seem as though men who are abusive or sexist can't help themselves, when in reality, they're making conscious choices to behave poorly. The problem comes when traits that society associates with masculinity become harmful and when they are discouraged in people of other genders. People besides cis men are equally as capable of doing or being these things.

An unfortunate side effect of toxic masculinity is the undervaluing and sometimes outright hatred of traditionally feminine traits, such as being emotional or compassionate. In cis men, they are seen as weaknesses; in trans men, they are seen as proof that they aren't "real" men; and in women, both cis and trans, as well as in nonbinary people, they are seen as reasons for oppression and violence.

Your Opinion Matters!

1. What are some other social constructs, and how do they affect society?
2. How can stereotypes limit people?
3. What are some examples of toxic masculinity in the media?

A HISTORY
OF REBELLION

Anthropologists suggest that gender inequality began as agriculture developed and people began accumulating resources such as food and land. During this time, women started to be treated like resources as well. The work women did and the children they had were valuable and turned into commodities, or economic goods. However, men were generally the ones profiting off of them.

The patriarchy was officially enforced when early civilizations started writing down their laws. The Code of Hammurabi, the earliest written code of law from ancient Babylon, contributed immensely to the oppression of women. Although it recognized women's rights to property and physical safety, "the code was a blow to women's sexual freedom. Husbands and fathers now owned the sexual reproduction of their wives and daughters. This meant that women could be put to death for adultery and that virginity was now a condition for marriage."[1] Control over a woman's sexual activity became a defining feature of the patriarchy because of inheritance and a new fixation on bloodline: If a man didn't know whether he had fathered the children his wife gave birth to, he couldn't be sure his amassed resources would

◀ The Code of Hammurabi was carved into this large, upright rock, which is known as a stele. The laws it set down seriously limited women's rights.

stay in his family after his death. Therefore, his wife was expected to have sex with only him for her entire life to ensure that any children she had were his.

Despite this shift in women's roles and rights, many women went against the expectations of their gender. Women were rulers, warriors, scientists, and thinkers of all kinds, even when it was unpopular or dangerous to live outside the social norm.

Early Rebels

Although men dominated most of the ancient world, some women—often upper-class or royal women—took power regardless of male disapproval. In ancient Egypt, women tended to be equal to men in terms of independence. They could marry and divorce freely, own property, travel alone, and earn their own money. They were only somewhat limited in their occupations; although there were many jobs they could take, they were excluded from positions of authority such as general, governor, and pharaoh. However, a few women did seize power and become rulers over the 3,000-year course of ancient Egyptian history: Hatshepsut, who ruled from 1473 to 1458 BCE; Nefertiti, who ruled from 1353 to 1336 BCE; and Cleopatra VII, who ruled from 51 to 30 BCE, are among the most well-known female rulers of Egypt. Although some, like Nefertiti, never assumed the title of pharaoh, a number of queens ruled alongside their husbands and continued to rule alone after the king's death.

In ancient Rome, women were defined by their roles as homemaker, wife, and mother. In many regards, they were often only slightly better off than slaves when it came to personal rights. A girl was considered her father's property until she married, at which time she became her husband's property. Similar to other nearby civilizations such as Babylon, Roman women's sexuality was strictly controlled. However, women did occasionally strike back against their society. One famous incident in 195 BCE involved the invasion of the Forum—an important meeting place for religious, political, and social activities—by a group of women

Hatshepsut, Queen of Egypt

Queen Hatshepsut began her reign as regent for her stepson, Thutmose III, who was too young to rule at the time. However, within seven years, she had assumed the mantle of pharaoh, a role typically reserved for men. As a way to gain public support for the unconventional way she'd taken the throne, she often had herself depicted with male features and a beard in the numerous statues she had erected. Calling herself "The Daughter of Re" and "His Majesty, Herself," she ruled for 15 years. Near the end of her reign, she had a pair of obelisks built at Karnak, a temple complex near Luxor, Egypt. An inscription in one reads, "Now my heart turns this way and that, as I think what the people will say—those who shall see my monuments in years to come, and who shall speak of what I have done."[1]

After her death, Thutmose finally ascended the throne. In a fit of rage at having been kept from what he considered rightfully his, he attempted to destroy all evidence of his stepmother and her very successful reign by destroying her statues and erasing her name from monuments. Thankfully, his plan did not succeed, and Hatshepsut's legacy as a true ruler of Egypt lives on to this day.

1. Quoted in Elizabeth B. Wilson, "The Queen Who Would Be King," *Smithsonian*, September 2006, www.smithsonianmag.com/history/the-queen-who-would-be-king-130328511.

Although in this statue Hatshepsut is wearing masculine clothes, it is one of the rare few to show her with feminine features.

in protest of a law that restricted how much gold and what colors they could wear. Livy, a Roman historian, described the event:

> The matrons, whom neither counsel nor shame nor their husbands' orders could keep at home, blockaded every street in the city and every entrance to the Forum. As the men came down to the Forum, the matrons besought them to let them, too, have back the luxuries they had enjoyed before, giving as their reason that the republic was thriving and that everyone's private wealth was increasing with every day. This crowd of women was growing daily, for now they were even gathering from the towns and villages. Before long they dared go up and solicit consuls, praetors, and other [government officials].[2]

The women eventually won the debate, and the law was officially revoked. However, as a whole, Roman women remained subject to the men who ruled their society.

Farther north, Celtic women enjoyed more freedom than most other women of the day. Women in the British Isles had rights similar to those of ancient Egyptian women: They could be landowners, had agency over who they married, and were even allowed to become warriors. Later, Scandinavian women in Viking tribes saw similar equality and explored, raided, and fought alongside men.

One of the most famous of these warrior women was the Celtic queen Boudicca, who led a rebellion against the Roman Empire after Emperor Nero stole her husband's land and humiliated her family. In 60 CE, her revolt destroyed three cities and left 80,000 Roman citizens dead. Although historians believe she poisoned herself after her eventual defeat, her willingness to go to war against the most powerful empire in the ancient world showcased the strength and determination of women at this time.

Education and Enlightenment

As the Roman Empire spread, so did its ideas about women. Not only were women expected to take care of the home, but they also lost their rights to property and personal freedom. Ancient Rome continued influencing gender politics throughout the Western world long after its collapse in 476 CE.

In Europe, where Roman influence was the most intense, women were wives and mothers—and little else. They were expected to be seen and not heard and had to obey their fathers and husbands at all times. They were also rarely educated. For young women from upper-class families, being taught simple reading and writing skills became a symbol of status, but lower-class women were likely to never be formally schooled in anything. Learning these skills led some upper-class women to begin writing works of their own—and, even more scandalously, publishing them for others to read. One such woman was Christine de Pisan. Born in 1364, she was a French-Italian poet and author who often wrote on the subjects of women's education and their roles in society. In *The Book of the City of Ladies*, de Pisan wrote, "Not all men (and especially the wisest) share the opinion that it is bad for women to be educated. But it is very true that many foolish men have claimed this because it displeased them that women knew more than they did."[3] Although she was unable to change the culture she lived in, she championed women in her writing until her death in 1430 and is considered one of the earliest feminist writers.

It wasn't until the late 1600s that more women began openly stepping outside their boundaries. It was during this time that Sir Isaac Newton published his laws of motion and John Locke published his theories about the human mind and its sense of self. These works and many others revolutionized science, mathematics, and philosophy, and the Age of Enlightenment began. This time period saw the development of the scientific method, the philosophy of rationalism, politics based on liberty, and many other concepts that have since become pillars of modern society.

With so many new ideas to be shared, reading and writing became more important than ever before. Throughout the 18th century, the publishing industry boomed, and not only

The Age of Enlightenment afforded women more opportunities for education, allowing women such as Marie-Ann Paulze Lavoisier (*shown here with her husband*) to make significant contributions to science, art, and literature in the late 18th and early 19th centuries.

in the subjects of science and philosophy. In the new age of reason, realistic fiction and reading for pleasure also became popular. Many of the most avid readers were women from upper-class families who wanted to read about their own lives rather than about fantasies. For the first time, there was demand for a woman's perspective. One of the most famous writers of the time, Margaret Cavendish, was unique because she didn't use a pen name to hide her gender. She wrote poems, prose romances, essays, and plays over the course of her career, and she openly criticized many of the great philosophers of the day, such as Thomas Hobbes and René Descartes.

Women also contributed to science during the Enlightenment, although many of their discoveries have been forgotten. The first time the word "scientist" was printed was in a review of Mary Somerville's *On the Connexion of the Physical Sciences*, which summarized physics, astronomy, meteorology, and geography. Somerville wrote nine total volumes on physical science while also running a household, in contrast to men of the day, who were able to focus solely on their work. Other important women of the time included Marie-Anne Paulze Lavoisier, a chemist who discovered the element oxygen with her husband and helped standardize the scientific method; Caroline Herschel, an astronomer who discovered eight comets; and Sophie Germain, a mathematician who contributed extensively to number theory and the study of elasticity in physics.

Driven by new liberty-based politics, both the American and French Revolutions took place at the end of the Enlightenment period. Although women tended to play supporting roles in the revolutions, they were sometimes found serving as nurses. Less commonly, some dressed as men in order to fight. During the French Revolution, in particular, women participated fully in the demonstrations and riots. As the French monarchy fell, women took the opportunity to advocate for educational opportunities and for social and political equality, although the results of their efforts were mixed.

The Domestic Sphere

As the spirit of revolution faded away and the 1800s marched on, women were once again shoved into what had become traditional gender roles—wife, mother, and caretaker. Since ancient times, men—and even some women—had taken the physical differences between men and women as a sign that they were inherently different in all areas of life. The ancient Greek philosopher Aristotle believed that men were the truest, best form of humanity. To him, women were merely deformed, corrupted versions of men and were therefore inferior. Although medical science had disproved this theory by the 19th century, the meaning behind it persisted into the industrial age and left women with few rights.

By the end of the 18th century, the dominating idea about gender roles revolved around the concept of separate spheres. Men occupied the public sphere, which included politics and working outside the home. Having a good public reputation became increasingly important, and maintaining this reputation required embodying gender roles such as dominance and rationality. Women, on the other hand, occupied the private or domestic sphere, which included family life and taking care of the home. They were expected to be hardworking, but only within the home, as well as patient, virtuous, and obedient. They couldn't vote, and although they were allowed to own property, women who lived alone or only with other women were looked down on. John Ruskin, an English writer of the era, outlined these separate spheres in his book *Sesame and Lilies*:

> The man's power is active, progressive, defensive. He is eminently the doer, the creator, the discoverer, the defender. His intellect is for speculation and invention; his energy for adventure, for war, and for conquest ... But the woman's power is for rule, not for battle,—and her intellect is not for invention or creation, but for sweet ordering, arrangement, and decision ... She must be enduringly, incorruptibly good; instinctively, infallibly wise—

After the American and French Revolutions, changing societal expectations forced women back into rigid, traditional gender roles that kept many of them in their homes for the next 150 years.

wise, not for self-development, but for [self-sacrifice]: wise, not that she may set herself above her husband, but that she many never fail from his side.[4]

Unfortunately, the rigid social norms of the time made abuse easy to get away with. The strict division between public and private life isolated women and made it difficult for them to seek help if they were being physically or sexually abused by their husbands or fathers. Not only was hitting women occasionally considered acceptable to keep women "in check," it was difficult for women to find help even if they were able to leave their situation. Although abusive lower-class men were often caught, social standing protected middle- and upper-class men even if strong evidence could be brought against them.

In worst-case scenarios, women who accused their husbands of abuse were said to be delusional. They were sometimes diagnosed with "female hysteria," a diagnosis used to explain any behavior outside the social norm, even when abuse was not involved. The signs of hysteria were what psychologists would now describe as symptoms of trauma or mental illness—anxiety, depression, insomnia, irritability, and loss of appetite—but doctors at the time believed they were symptoms of sexual deprivation, and many doctors sexually assaulted their patients in the name of a cure. Many women were sent away to asylums because of their "hysteria," and they were only allowed to return home once they "recovered" and were willing to go back into the seclusion of the home and their social roles.

First-Wave Feminism

The first wave of feminism in America formally began in July 1848 in Seneca Falls, New York. Women's rights activist Elizabeth Cady Stanton and antislavery activist Lucretia Mott organized the Seneca Falls Convention to officially declare the goals of the women's rights movement. About 300 people attended, 200 of them women. On July 19, Stanton opened the convention by reading the "Declaration of Sentiments," a document meant to outline the rights that women had long been denied. Echoing the Declaration of Independence, the Declaration of Sentiments began, "We hold these truths to be self-evident; that all men and women are created equal," and it continued:

> The history of mankind is a history of repeated injuries and usurpations [takeovers] on the part of man toward woman, having in direct object the establishment of an absolute tyranny over her … He has never permitted her to exercise her inalienable right to the elective franchise. He has compelled her to submit to laws, in the formation of which she had no voice … He has made her, if married, in the eye of the law, civilly dead. He has taken from her all right in property, even to the wages she earns.[5]

"Elective franchise," or the right to vote, was the central issue of first-wave feminism. Also known as suffrage, the right to vote was a right that few women had enjoyed. Before the colonization of America, Native American women were generally considered political equals and had equal power when it came to making tribal decisions, but the US government did not adopt this system. For brief, separate periods, women in the Massachusetts Bay Colony and the state of New Jersey were allowed to vote, but by the mid-1800s, women's suffrage was a controversial topic. Gaining the right to vote would push women firmly into the public sphere of politics, and this was unacceptable to many men and women alike. While men stood to potentially lose their position at the top of society, women who opposed the movement felt that the idea of femininity would be lost if they took up "manly" causes.

While the suffrage movement was emerging, the abolitionist, or antislavery, movement was growing as well, and there was much overlap between the two causes. However, although the women's rights movement had its roots in the abolitionist movement, first-wave feminism often excluded black women and other women of color. Stanton, in particular, was unconcerned with the struggles of black women. Although she claimed to fight for all women, "when she said 'women' ... she primarily had in mind women much like herself: white, middle-class, culturally if not religiously protestant, propertied, well-educated."[6] The exclusion of people of color continued to varying degrees throughout the evolution of the feminist movement, and it still affects feminism today.

Two decades after the Seneca Falls Convention, in the wake of the American Civil War, the suffrage movement split between two organizations: the National Woman Suffrage Association (NWSA) and the American Woman Suffrage Association (AWSA). They were divided on the best way to achieve their goals. The NWSA, founded by Stanton and Susan B. Anthony, another social reformer and women's rights activist, wanted suffrage on a federal, or national, level so that all women across the country would have the right to vote. However, it also opposed the 15th Amendment, which had given black men the right to vote before white women. The AWSA, founded by abolitionist Lucy Stone, sought to change state laws rather than involve the federal government. A change came in 1890, though, as more and more middle-class women began joining social causes such as charitable organizations and the temperance, or anti-alcohol, movement. With more women becoming involved in life outside the home, the suffrage movement had more leverage, and the two organizations became one: the National American Woman Suffrage Association (NAWSA). For three decades, the NAWSA worked tirelessly to change the country's mind about suffrage, and on August 26, 1920, the 19th Amendment gave women across the country the right to vote.

Second-Wave Feminism

The second wave of feminism gained momentum in the 1960s, a time when social change was happening fast. Sometimes called the women's liberation movement, second-wave feminism grew out of the civil rights movement, which worked toward achieving equal rights for black people, and the anti-Vietnam War movement, in which people advocated for peace and opposed US involvement in the Vietnam War. Second-wave feminism demanded freedom from oppression under the patriarchy. History professor Martha Rampton pointed out that the influences of these other movements changed feminism for the better:

> *Whereas the first wave of feminism was generally propelled by middle class, Western, cisgender, white women, the second phase drew in women of color and developing nations, seeking sisterhood and solidarity, claiming "Women's struggle is class struggle." Feminists spoke of women as a social class and coined phrases such as "the personal is political" and "identity politics" in an effort to demonstrate that race, class, and gender oppression are all related.*[7]

Second-wave feminists often rejected all elements of femininity. After a protest at the Miss America 1969 pageant where feminists burned bras, makeup, hairspray, and other feminine products in a trash can, they were commonly called "bra-burners" and became known for refusing to conform to traditional gender roles.

Some pinpoint the development of oral contraceptives, or birth control pills, as the beginning of second-wave feminism. Approved by the US Food and Drug Administration (FDA) in 1960, "the pill," as it came to be called, gave women the option to have sex without worrying as much about getting pregnant. This choice allowed them to pursue other life goals before or instead of raising a family. Although some criticized the pill for encouraging young, unmarried women to have sex, it was originally more often used by married women who already had children and didn't want more. Nevertheless, this convenient form of birth control put women's reproduction choices exclusively under their control and started what became known as the sexual revolution. The women's liberation movement promoted taking charge of one's sexual behavior, and many women did.

Out of the civil rights movement came the Civil Rights Act of 1964, which prohibited discrimination against people in the workplace based on race, nationality, or religion. Title VII of the act also protected people against discrimination based on sex, which opened many career opportunities for women that they had never had before. In addition, a year earlier, Betty Friedan had published her wildly popular book *The Feminine Mystique*. In this book, she openly criticized the idea that women should only find happiness and fulfillment in being wives and mothers. The combination of these

The Flapper

In the 1920s, in the wake of the 19th Amendment, young women began taking the ideas of freedom and equality and applying them to how they dressed and what they did. Short, bobbed hairstyles came into fashion, skirts rose to a scandalous knee length, and speakeasies—illegal bars in the time of alcohol prohibition in America—became popular hangouts for women as well as men. The media of the time portrayed so-called "flappers" as wild, dangerous girls. They smoked cigarettes, drank alcohol, went on unchaperoned dates, and generally ignored what was expected of women at the time.

For most, being a flapper was not a deliberately feminist choice. After World War I, Western culture suffered a major upheaval—the violence and senselessness of the war had taught people that life was short. Also, political scandals showed that institutions such as the government could be corrupt. According to Judith Mackrell, a writer for the *Guardian*, these changes affected how women saw themselves in the postwar era:

If the politics of feminism seemed less important to the "flapper generation", this was partly because young women were taking the struggle for freedom into their personal lives. Ideas of duty, sacrifice and the greater good had been debunked by the recent war; for this generation, morality resided in being true to one's self, not to a cause. Towards the end of the decade, some feminists would argue that women's great achievement in the 20s was learning to value their individuality.[1]

1. Judith Mackrell, "The 1920s: 'Young Women Took the Struggle for Freedom into Their Personal Lives,'" *Guardian*, February 5, 2018, www.theguardian.com/lifeandstyle/2018/feb/05/the-1920s-young-women-took-the-struggle-for-freedom-into-their-personal-lives.

two things—the publication and popularity of *The Feminine Mystique* and Title VII—motivated many women to join the workforce. In 1960, about 38 percent of women worked, but by 1970, about 43 percent did, and by 1980, almost half of all women had a job outside the home.

After the cultural shift caused by World War I and the 19th amendment, the flapper became a symbol for women's newfound freedom. Shown here is Clara Bow, an actress who helped popularize the classic image of the flapper.

DON'T BE A CLOWN TAKE WOMEN ♀ SERIOUSLY ♀

Like the feminists who came before them, second-wave feminists weren't afraid to demand the rights they deserved.

The Gay Liberation Movement

The 1970s saw the rise of the gay liberation movement, which consisted of homosexual, bisexual, and gender-nonconforming people fighting for their rights and recognition in mainstream society. Most cite the Stonewall riots as the beginning of the movement. On June 28, 1969, police entered the Stonewall Inn, a gay bar in New York City, and began beating up patrons and arresting employees for selling alcohol without a license. This had become a common occurrence and was seen by the gay community as simply an excuse to harass them. In response, patrons threw bricks and lit the bar on fire, setting off a series of full-blown riots that went on for five days.

After the Stonewall riots, the gay community came together to fight for equality. The next year, on June 28, the first gay pride parade took place in New York City, and as with the feminist movement, organizations such as the Gay Liberation Front began demanding radical social change to erase homophobia. However, although transgender and nonbinary people had always been a part of the movement, the community became known only as the LGB (lesbian, gay, bisexual) community in the 1980s. The "T" for trans was not added until the 1990s.

In 1966, Friedan helped found the National Organization for Women (NOW) and became its first president. NOW's goal was to "bring women into full participation in the mainstream of American society now, exercising all the privileges and responsibilities thereof in truly equal partnership with men."[8] Its members fought to uphold Title VII; lobbied for abortion rights, which dealt with to a woman's right to end a pregnancy; and pushed the Equal Rights Amendment (ERA), a constitutional amendment guaranteeing women's rights, through Congress. Although the ERA was passed in Congress in 1972, it didn't receive approval from the necessary 38 states and was not adopted into law. However, in January 2020, the 38th state, Virginia, ratified, or approved, the amendment. As of early 2020, Congress is debating it, although experts are unsure of whether it can gain enough support in the Senate to pass. Supreme Court Justice Ruth Bader Ginsburg has suggested that, rather than passing the ERA, lawmakers should start over and write a new, updated amendment to be ratified by the states.

NOW and much of the women's liberation movement tended, like their predecessors, to focus heavily on the struggles of middle-class, white women. Poor women, who worked outside the home long before Title VII, and women of color, who experienced both sexism and racism, were often left out of the conversation. Discussions about gender and sexuality, too, tended to be binary—women and men, gay and straight—and left out everyone else.

Third-Wave Feminism

Powered by postmodernism and the newly popular World Wide Web, the third wave of feminism started in the mid-1990s. The philosophy of postmodernism still shapes feminism today. It asks that people question their beliefs and thoroughly examine social norms and constructs, and in the 1990s, it caused a new generation to reshape what feminism meant. Rampton wrote, "The 'grrls' of the third wave stepped onto the stage as strong and empowered, [rejecting] victimization and defining feminine beauty for themselves as subjects, not as objects of a sexist patriarchy."[9] To the shock of their foremothers, many third-wave feminists wore lipstick, high heels, and push-up bras, and they sometimes embraced derogatory words for women.

Third-wave feminists were the daughters of second-wave feminism; born in and around the 1970s, their role models were sometimes quite literally their mothers. Raised with strong examples of female empowerment and the expectation of high achievement, the third wave went after the remaining barriers of sexism, racism, and classism. As the internet and celebrity culture made them more aware of how women were portrayed in the media, many women reclaimed and subverted feminine stereotypes. Makeup and high heels were worn for the sake of fashion, not for the sake of men. The women of the era aspired

Modern feminism has reclaimed the trappings of femininity that the second wave discarded and turned them into symbols of female independence and power.

to be powerful and assertive, in charge of their sexuality and how they were perceived, and free from the expectations of men.

Discussions about gender became more nuanced. Third-wave feminists acknowledged that there were no such things as inherently "feminine" and "masculine" traits, only traits assigned to certain genders. Meanwhile, the LGB community finally recognized its transgender and nonbinary members with the addition of the "T" to LGBT. Although gender nonconformity had always been around, it had often been hidden from public view or played up as an artistic statement. Third-wave feminism made room for people to be whoever they wanted to be, whenever they wanted.

Your Opinion Matters!

1. How has the history of sexism and misogyny set the stage for today's society?
2. What can we learn from the way women of the past were treated?
3. What were the central issues of the first, second, and third waves of feminism?

FOURTH-WAVE FEMINISM

Although some disagree, many believe that the fourth wave of feminism began around 2012. As social media became a deeply ingrained part of life, women around the world could connect and share their experiences in new ways. One of the fourth wave's defining features is feminism as a global movement. While the third wave was about individualism and never truly acknowledged itself as a collective social movement, the fourth wave encourages presenting feminism as a united front—at least in most situations.

Although there are many topics that modern feminists tend to agree about—the wage gap, rape culture, the unrealistic standards and regulations set on women's bodies—there are also many questions that have led to divisions within the movement. How should these problems be solved? Who should be included? How should people define themselves as we move toward gender equality? Many different people, including people outside the feminist movement, believe they have the answers, but it will take a long time to find lasting solutions.

The Effect of Social Media

Social media, according to journalist Natashya Gutierrez, has "given women around the world a voice. It has shed light on

 Some subway cars in Japan are designated "women only" because men frequently take advantage of crowded cars to grope women, or touch them inappropriately.

women's issues that were not previously discussed and enhances conversations around topics not covered by mainstream media. It triggers participation for real-life campaigns. And in many cases, these seemingly simple hashtags have instigated change."[1] The connectivity of social media has brought global issues to the forefront of feminist discussions.

For a long time, Western feminists focused only on the problems faced by Western society, but fourth-wave feminism is concerned with how all people are affected by patriarchy within their own cultures. Social media platforms such as Twitter, Instagram, and Facebook have allowed women all over the world to share their experiences, start communities, and expose injustices. In Middle Eastern and South Asian countries such as Saudi Arabia and Pakistan, feminists have used social media to bring attention to the issues of male guardianship, which requires a man to give his permission before a woman can make any decisions, and honor killings, which are used as punishment for women and girls who act out and bring "dishonor" to their families. In East Asia, the #MeToo movement has opened a conversation about the massive sexual harassment problem in South Korea, China, and other countries in the region.

However, speaking up over social media is not always a good thing. While it's important for these issues to be seen by the world in order to make changes, many women get in trouble for exposing the misogyny in their countries. In Saudi Arabia, many activists have been arrested over the past several years because of online protests, and in South Korea, women have been accused by the Justice Department of lying when they share their stories about sexual harassment. In these cases, having the world's attention can force these countries to make changes, but it can also endanger activists if individuals or the government wish to retaliate.

Visibility Grows

Over the past decade, feminist issues such as sexual harassment, the wage gap, and many others have become popular topics in the media. As feminists have made themselves more visible to the public eye through social media, both the news and entertainment

#MeToo

In 2017, actress Alyssa Milano tweeted, "If you've been sexually harassed or assaulted write 'me too' as a reply to this tweet,"[1] and her tweet quickly went viral. The #MeToo movement is about supporting survivors of sexual violence and giving them the space to tell their stories if they choose to. In the first 24 hours after Milano's tweet, the hashtag was used more than 12 million times on Twitter, Facebook, and Snapchat, and it spurred a wave of women coming forward to accuse their attackers.

However, the #MeToo movement was actually founded in 2006 by Tarana Burke, a civil rights activist. She created Just Be Inc., a nonprofit organization focused on helping survivors of sexual assault and harassment. After #MeToo went viral, "some women of color noted pointedly that the longtime effort by Ms. Burke, who is black, had not received support over the years from prominent white feminists."[2] Although some effort was made to include Burke after the hashtag went viral, this controversy went largely unnoticed in the media, and Milano is still often credited with the creation of the movement.

1. Alyssa Milano (@Alyssa_Milano), "If you've been sexually harassed," Twitter, October 15, 2017, 1:21 a.m., twitter.com/Alyssa_Milano/status/919659438700670976.

2. Sandra E. Garcia, "The Woman Who Created #MeToo Long Before Hashtags," *New York Times*, October 20, 2017, www.nytimes.com/2017/10/20/us/me-too-movement-tarana-burke.html.

industries have turned their focus on feminism. Many celebrities—including Emma Watson, Beyoncé, and Ariana Grande—have come out in support of the movement and helped popularize it.

The visibility of feminism is also due in part to the increased visibility of the LGBTQ+ community. Feminism and the LGBTQ+ movement often go hand in hand because of both communities' focus on gender, sexuality, and equality. Increased exposure has led to enormous growth within the LGBTQ+ movement, and as it has expanded, so has its acronym and terminology. With names ranging from LGBTTQQIAAP (lesbian, gay, bisexual, transgender, transsexual, queer, questioning, intersex, asexual, ally, pansexual) to simply "queer" or "gay," the community is most often referred to as LGBTQ+, with the plus standing in to include multitudes of genders and sexual identities.

Despite the power that visibility gives feminism, some feminists believe that the movement's growing popularity may actually not amount to much. Feminism is not meant to be popular—like any social movement, the point of feminism is to make people uncomfortable with the status quo, and celebrities, by the nature of their jobs, can't make people too uncomfortable without risking their careers. Making feminism high profile, then, may rob it of its impact. However, others believe that introducing feminism to the mainstream is a huge step toward making lasting changes to the culture. The more people know about it, the more people are likely to agree with it and seek to shift society in a feminist direction.

The Wage Gap

For every dollar a white man makes, a white woman in a similar career makes 80 cents. The gap is even more pronounced among most women of color—black women make 63 cents, Latinas make 54 cents, and Native American women make 57 cents for every dollar a white man earns. Despite the workplace equality guaranteed by Title VII, companies are often able to find ways around it. Many believe the problem lies in the hiring and promotion processes: Managers may have a gender bias, whether they know it or not, and may hire women at lower starting salaries than men. Additionally, even when women and men make the same amount at hiring, men are more likely to be promoted into higher paying senior positions. The existence of the pay gap has been proven by research and data from sources such as the US Census Bureau, but polls show that many Americans—46 percent of men and 30 percent of women—believe the issue is made up.

There are many complex issues that contribute to both the wage gap and the myths behind it. For example, many people believe women earn less because men work harder and longer hours.

The Corporate Side of Equal Rights

In recent years, companies such as Dove, Always, CoverGirl, and Gillette have begun using feminism in their marketing campaigns. Although some people see this as nothing more than a cheap trick, others see it as a mark of the changing times. Changing individuals' minds is important, but it means very little if the culture doesn't change. Whether or not a marketing team actually feels strongly about feminist issues, it's still important for people to see those messages being supported.

Movies such as *Captain Marvel*, *Wonder Woman*, and the *Star Wars* series also work to change the culture. Recently, the film industry realized that female viewers were a huge market that was going untapped, especially in regard to genres such as science fiction and superhero films. Although women were going to see these movies regardless of the gender of the lead, making mainstream movies with feminist values sends the message that women's stories are equally as valuable as men's.

However, feminists often criticize these campaigns for ultimately being nonthreatening to the patriarchy. "Popular feminism," as author Sarah Banet-Weiser calls it, does very little to question or change the underlying structures that make sentiments such as "be confident" and "love your body" necessary. "I think that many, many women and many men actually get a lot out of patriarchy," Banet-Weiser said in an interview about her book *Empowered: Popular Feminism and Popular Misogyny*. "But many women also want to challenge certain parts of it, but not all of it. Popular feminism allows them to kind of do that, to feel like 'I'm confident, I have power, but I'm not actually going to go and try to appeal to the state to change wage discrimination or racism.'"[1]

1. Quoted in Rebecca Jennings, "Why 'Feminist' Advertising Doesn't Make Us Better Feminists," Vox, November 5, 2018, www.vox.com/the-goods/2018/11/5/18056004/feminist-advertising-empowered-sarah-banet-weiser.

However, care of the household overwhelmingly still falls to women, which means many aren't able to stay late at work or come in on weekends; they're expected to go home, make dinner, take care of

Despite laws set in place to prevent it, women still make significantly less then men in similar careers.

the kids, clean the house, and do other chores that allow men to focus their full attention on their paying jobs. Industries that reward working longer continuous hours, such as banking, have some of the highest wage gaps. Furthermore, there's no evidence to support the idea that men work harder or are better at their jobs. In fact, many women excel in their careers. Other complex myths include the idea that men have more education than women and that men are more likely to choose careers that pay more. As Robin Schwartz, managing partner and human resources director at the job-finding website Career Igniter, explained, "The wage gap isn't just about a man being paid more than … women for the same job, it's about ensuring women are given equal opportunity and motivation to excel in higher paying career fields."[2]

Inequality in the workplace is set up by inequality in school. Women around the world are often denied the right to go to college, and sometimes they're denied education of any kind. However, even in countries that provide equal opportunities for education, women are underrepresented in science, technology, engineering, and math (STEM) fields and in high-ranking executive positions, which are some of the highest paying careers. The same problem is seen among people of color, and particularly among women of color. Katherine B. Coffman, a Harvard Business School professor, noted that these issues arise because of what women and people of color are taught to believe about themselves—namely, that they're less qualified for higher paying jobs:

> *Our beliefs about ourselves are important in shaping all kinds of important decisions, such as what colleges we apply to, which career paths we choose, and whether we are willing to contribute ideas in the workplace or try to compete for a promotion. If talented women in STEM aren't confident, they might not even look at those fields in the first place. It's all about how good we think we*

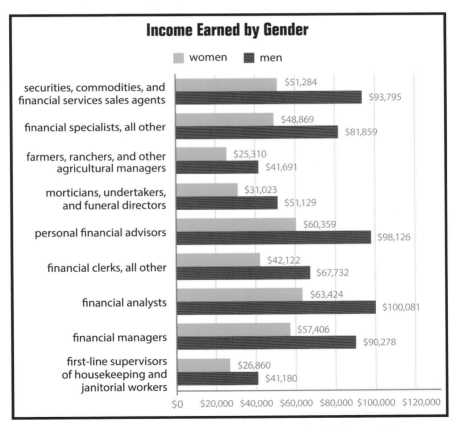

Income Earned by Gender

women / men

	women	men
securities, commodities, and financial services sales agents	$51,284	$93,795
financial specialists, all other	$48,869	$81,859
farmers, ranchers, and other agricultural managers	$25,310	$41,691
morticians, undertakers, and funeral directors	$31,023	$51,129
personal financial advisors	$60,359	$98,126
financial clerks, all other	$42,122	$67,732
financial analysts	$63,424	$100,081
financial managers	$57,406	$90,278
first-line supervisors of housekeeping and janitorial workers	$26,860	$41,180

$0 $20,000 $40,000 $60,000 $80,000 $100,000 $120,000

The gender wage gap is extremely wide in certain fields, as this information from *Business Insider* shows.

are, especially when we ask ourselves, "What does it make sense for me to pursue?"[3]

Multiple studies have also found another reason that women are often paid less: children. "We note that children may have two conceptually different effects on labor market outcomes," wrote the authors of a study done in Denmark in 2018. "One is a pre-child effect of anticipated fertility: women may invest less in education or select family friendly career paths in anticipation of motherhood. The other is a post-child effect of realized fertility: women changing their hours worked, occupation, sector, firm, etc., in response to actual motherhood."[4] Feminists don't believe women should stop having children; instead, they criticize the expectation that women should put having children ahead of any of their other goals, including achieving career success.

Violence and Rape Culture

Violence against women has been a problem throughout history. In particular, feminists tend to focus on intimate partner, or domestic, violence and sexual violence because they're the most common. About 30 percent of women worldwide, or one out of every three, have experienced intimate partner violence, meaning they have been assaulted by someone they were in a relationship with. This can be physical, sexual, or psychological abuse. Trans and nonbinary people are also at risk for intimate partner violence, with 54 percent reporting that they've experienced it before.

Sexual violence, including rape and sexual harassment, is a common topic in the media today. With the spread of the #MeToo movement and the accusations brought against some of the most powerful men in the entertainment and business industries, what feminists call rape culture has been brought to the public's attention. Rape culture refers to the social acceptance and normalization of sexual abuse. Rape culture is perpetuated, or upheld, in many different ways. Only about 31 percent of rapes are reported to the police, for example, because the police only follow through with an arrest about 6 percent of the time.

The #MeToo movement has brought much-needed attention to the widespread issue of sexual harassment and rape that permeates most world cultures.

Rape culture is also seen in victim-blaming, or when survivors of assault are told that they brought their assault on themselves. Rape victims are often told that what they were wearing or what they were doing (walking home alone, drinking at a bar, flirting with someone, etc.) is the reason they were raped. This is harmful not only because it can re-traumatize the survivor or make them feel worse, but also because it removes fault and responsibility for the rape from the rapist. Slut-shaming, or being socially punished for being sexual, also comes into play in victim-blaming and is part of rape culture. Slut-shaming generally only happens to women, and being labeled a "slut" is often used as justification for rape or sexual harassment. However, author and *HuffPost* reporter Leora Tanenbaum pointed out that "it actually makes no difference if a girl or woman is sexually active or even utters any expression of sexuality: she can be called to task simply because she is female."[5] Feminists believe this is an expression of the patriarchy attempting to control women's bodies.

Some people claim rape culture doesn't exist. They argue that rape and sexual harassment are considered far from the norm. However, the statistics suggest otherwise. Studies show that 20 percent of women have survived rape or attempted rape, and that 17 percent of men have been sexually abused before they turn 18. These numbers alone suggest that rape is more common than some believe. "If so many millions of women were getting carjacked or kidnapped, we'd call it a public crisis," said author Jaclyn Friedman. "That we accept it as normal, even inevitable, is all the evidence I need."[6]

"My Body, My Choice"

Bodily autonomy is the subject of intense debate in today's society. Having bodily autonomy means no one has a say in what someone does with their body except that person; family, friends, and lawmakers have no right to tell someone what they can and can't do to and with their own body. Feminists believe that the government has a responsibility to protect people's bodily autonomy, especially when it comes to the topic of abortion. People with this view call themselves pro-choice. People who oppose abortion call themselves pro-life. Sometimes pro-life people mistakenly call the other side pro-abortion, but this is not an accurate label because pro-choice people don't believe everyone should have an abortion; they simply think the choice should be available and the person who's pregnant should be the only one who gets to make it.

From the mid-1800s to 1973, getting an abortion was illegal across the United States, except in some cases where the procedure would save the person's life. Because of this, secret and illegal abortions known as "back-alley" abortions were common, but they were life threatening since they were often performed in unsanitary environments by people with little training. However, in 1973, the Supreme Court ruled in the case *Roe v. Wade* that restrictive state regulation of abortion was unconstitutional because criminalizing abortion violated Americans' right to privacy. Between 1972 and 1974, the number of illegal abortions dropped from 130,000 to

This pro-choice monument in Washington, DC, is devoted to the victims of illegal abortions.

17,000, and the number of deaths from these illegal procedures dropped from 39 to 5 a year.

The Guttmacher Institute, a reproductive health research organization, concluded, "The abortion rate is 37 per 1,000 women in countries that prohibit abortion altogether or allow it only to save a woman's life, and 34 per 1,000 in countries that allow abortion without restriction as to reason—a difference that is not significant."[7] Although the rates of abortion are almost the same whether it's legal or not, the chance of surviving the procedure is much higher when abortion is legal. Ultimately, feminists believe that saving people's lives should be the top priority.

Not all feminists support abortion. Many believe adoption is a better solution to unwanted pregnancies. However, most feminists will agree that the option to have an abortion is still important and that the right to choose is one that should be protected. In 2019, both Georgia and Alabama prepared anti-abortion bills that would take away the bodily autonomy of pregnant people in their states. These bills were known as "heartbeat bills" because they outlawed abortion after a fetus's heartbeat could be detected. Many people protested because this occurs at around six weeks—so early into a pregnancy that many women aren't even aware they're pregnant yet. The purpose of heartbeat bills is to effectively ban abortion while still complying with *Roe v. Wade*. Both bills were blocked by their states' courts.

Reactionary Attitudes

Although many feminist goals would help men as well as women, cis men often feel as if they will lose something if they are no longer in power. Because of this, some men organize against women—and feminists in particular—to try and prevent them from "taking away" what they think society owes them. The most common name for these people is men's rights activists (MRAs).

Warren Farrell, the father of the men's rights movement, "has made the case that the primary victims of gender-based discrimination are men—casualties of a society that relies on their sacrifices while ignoring their suffering."[8] Paul Elam, the founder of the MRA website A Voice For Men, said, "Society piles complete and total responsibility on men for its existence … Almost all the sacrifice, of blood and sweat and of life that is required to keep the world turning, to keep us living in relative comfort and safety, is male sacrifice. Women won't do it. Women can't do it."[9] However, feminists point out that this is an incomplete view of society. Firstly, it ignores the fact that women have repeatedly sought the same rights and responsibilities as men—such as the right to work outside the home, join the military, and vote—and have either been disregarded or have won those rights after decades of difficult fighting. Secondly, it ignores feminism's focus on how the patriarchy affects everyone, including cis men. Most feminists will openly acknowledge the problems of the high male suicide rate, the dismissal of male sexual assault, and the gender biases that take children away from their fathers in court because women are assumed to be better caregivers.

Thirdly, MRAs ignore women's suffering and deny their group's contributions to it. Not only do MRAs tend to be misogynistic online, some of them have taken their rage out on people in real life. One of the most famous instances of this was the case of Elliot Rodger, who killed six and injured thirteen in a 2014 shooting that ended with his suicide. The 137-page manifesto he left behind was a tirade against women who refused to date him. Since then, Rodger has become an MRA hero, and other self-described "incels"—short for "involuntary celibates," a term some men use to describe themselves when they feel women are not giving them the sexual activity they believe they are owed as men—have carried out murders and rapes in the name of men's rights.

Your Opinion Matters!

1. Do you think feminism would have changed if the internet hadn't been invented?

2. What are some examples of rape culture beyond the ones mentioned previously?

3. Do you consider yourself pro-choice or pro-life? Explain your answer.

CHAPTER FOUR

INTERSECTIONAL EQUALITY

Although the word "intersectional" wasn't introduced to feminism until 1989, the idea began circulating years earlier. In the 19th century, activist Anna J. Cooper—a member of the Black Liberation political movement—wrote about the intersection of race and gender in her book *A Voice from the South: By a Black Woman of the South*. She advocated for the education of black women—a controversial subject in 1892—and argued that the women's suffrage movement would create a political environment open to desegregation and racial equality. Later, in 1981, activist Angela Davis wrote about the many ways in which racism prevented gender equality. Her book *Women, Race, and Class* examined women's suffrage, a movement dominated by middle-class white women, and how it ignored the needs of working-class black women.

Acknowledgement of these issues is known today as intersectionality, or a focus on "the complex, cumulative way in which the effects of multiple forms of discrimination combine, overlap, or intersect."[1] These forms of discrimination stem from problems such as racism, transphobia, homophobia, ableism, and classism. Intersectional feminism attempts to address these issues and strives to understand how they intersect both with each other and with sexism.

◀ Intersectional feminists care about racial issues, such as a justice system that disproportionly punishes black people for minor crimes.

Race

Racism is the discrimination against or hatred of someone because of their race or ethnic background. Experts on race theory claim that Western culture suffers from institutional, or systemic, racism, meaning that, like the patriarchy, racism is an engrained part of the culture. Institutional racism keeps power in the hands of white people through stereotypes and biases and deprives people of color of resources and opportunities.

Racism and sexism are intertwined—in some ways, they are inseparably linked. As activist and writer Julia Serano explained, "A woman of color doesn't face racism and sexism separately; the sexism she faces is often racialized, and the racism she faces is often sexualized."[2] For example, people of color, especially black and Latinx individuals, are often stereotyped as being sexually aggressive, so they're sometimes accused of being more likely to assault someone or cheat on their partner. This also makes black and Latina women more likely to be victim-blamed if someone assaults them. On the other hand, some people of color, such as East and Southeast Asian people, are stereotyped as being weak and submissive, making them targets for violence. Women of color also often make less money than white women and are more likely to have their medical issues be dismissed by a doctor as "all in their head" instead of being treated.

"White feminism" is the opposite of intersectional feminism. It tends to ignore problems faced by marginalized groups besides white women, especially those faced by women of color. White feminists sometimes feel upset and take it very personally if they're excluded from organizations or events that center the issues faced by women of color, even though, for a long time, women of color were excluded from feminist discussions despite the feminist movement's roots in the abolitionist movement. Even second-wave feminism, which was significantly more inclusive than the first wave, was led by many white women who didn't recognize that the issues they were talking about only applied to people like them. Betty Friedan, for instance, wrote *The Feminine Mystique* about the struggle housewives were having finding fulfillment when they were discouraged from working outside the home. However, "she failed to realize that women from less privileged backgrounds, often poor and non-white, already worked outside the home to support their families. Friedan's suggestion, then, was applicable only to a particular sub-group of women (white middle-class Western housewives). But it was mistakenly taken to apply to all women's lives."[3]

One example of white feminism is the criticism of the 2020 Super Bowl halftime show. Latina performers Shakira and Jennifer Lopez put on a show that featured singing, dancing, feats of athleticism, and sparkly outfits that were designed to look good while allowing the dancers freedom to perform. Many people loved the show. However, many others—some who identified as feminists, and some who didn't—felt it was inappropriate. They said Shakira and Lopez revealed too much skin and danced in a way that was too sexual for children to see. Many white feminists expressed a desire for the performers to cover up and dance differently, arguing that they wanted people to take women seriously for their intelligence rather than their bodies. Many of these same people didn't criticize Adam Levine's shirtless performance at the previous year's Super Bowl halftime show or Lady Gaga's bodysuit and bare stomach in 2017. Some of these critics had even talked in the past about a desire to desexualize the naked female body.

Intersectional feminists pointed out that it seemed as though these white feminists had a problem with the fact that most of the dancers on the halftime stage were people of color. They noted that singer Taylor Swift had worn similar outfits at performances and that Shakira and Lopez's clothing didn't reveal any more skin than the outfits athletes such as gymnasts and figure skaters wear. The "sexual" dancing was actually traditional in many Latin American cultures, and although Lopez danced on a pole—something many people associate with strippers—she didn't remove any of her clothes. While white women are generally praised for being comfortable with their bodies, women of color tend to be shamed for the same thing.

Today, few feminists who fall into the category of white feminism identify as such; many, in fact, call themselves intersectional feminists. However, women of color find that in many "intersection-al" feminist groups, they fill minority spots and are often ignored or accused of being divisive when they try to discuss issues that are particular to their race or ethnicity.

Gender and Sexual Orientation

LGBTQ+ people are often discriminated against because who they are, who they are attracted to, and how they express themselves frequently go against traditional social norms.

Since the LGBTQ+ movement has become more visible in the past few decades, many people have learned to embrace masculine and feminine traits regardless of their assigned sex and gender, and many more have joined the community. However, some people who are invested in the current power structure don't approve of letting people express themselves however they want in terms of gender. Nonbinary and trans people often experience sexism and misogyny from these people even when they don't identify as feminine. By breaking gender barriers, they threaten the patriarchy regardless of their identity, so they sometimes face discrimination and violence even worse than that directed toward cis women.

Assumptions about gender roles also affect people who aren't heterosexual. Gay men and men who are attracted to more than one gender are often stereotyped as being negatively feminine. Lesbians and other women who are attracted to women are often stereotyped as being too masculine. Because of Western culture's preoccupation with sexual purity, people who are attracted to multiple genders are often stereotyped as being promiscuous or unfaithful. Obviously, sometimes these stereotypes can be true—some gay men enjoy fashion and makeup, some lesbians embrace the term "butch," and some bisexual people enjoy dating many people—but these assumptions can be harmful if they're expected to be the norm and, at the same time, are also ridiculed or used as reasons for hate.

Asexual people—those who don't experience sexual attraction—also suffer under the patriarchy. Men are often expected to be obsessed with sex, so asexual men are sometimes seen as going against nature. Asexual women are similarly seen as unnatural,

More and more people are leaving behind traditional gender roles and expressing their gender identity however they choose.

but for different reasons. Toxic masculinity states that all women should be sexually available to men at all times. This is why even lesbians, who have no interest in men, are fetishized, and why some men become verbally or physically abusive when a woman rejects their advances. Asexual women sometimes inspire this kind of outrage because they are assumed to be sexually unavailable by nature.

Disability Rights

One area of inequality that is often overlooked is the issue of disability rights. More than 1 billion people on Earth have a disability, but many live under limiting circumstances and aren't given the opportunities and accommodations they need to lead productive, happy lives. Even in the United States, people with mental and physical disabilities continue to have to fight for rights such as equal education and health care. They sometimes aren't allowed to live independently even if they want to, and many are left homeless, institutionalized, or stuck in the criminal justice system.

gender essentialism and exclude trans women from feminist discussions and spaces based on the false idea that they are not "real" women. Many TERFs argue that trans people are shining a spotlight on gender when the goal should be to abolish it. This argument is similar to one that says people who talk about racism are drawing too much attention to the issue of race and that the goal should instead be to ignore race. Both arguments ignore the very real effects gender and race have on people's lives. Many TERFs consider "TERF" a slur or a form of hate speech, but other feminists argue that it's an accurate description of their beliefs.

Some question whether TERFs count as feminists at all. Even the woman who coined the term, Viv Smythe, wondered if it was an accurate description. She wrote, "After a bit more reading, I think the trans-exclusionary set should better be described as TES, with the S standing for separatists. A lot of the positions that are presented seem far too essentialist to be adequately described as feminist, let alone radical feminist."[1] Radfems are revolutionary in nature, but the radical feminist perspective doesn't necessarily call for essentialism or the exclusion of trans people.

1. Viv Smythe, "I'm Credited with Having Coined the Word 'Terf'. Here's How It Happened," *Guardian*, November 28, 2018, www.theguardian.com/commentisfree/2018/nov/29/im-credited-with-having-coined-the-acronym-terf-heres-how-it-happened.

Although disability rights and gender equality are two different missions, they're similar in many ways, and intersectional feminists consider them related. "Feminist and disability rights are born from a similar cloth," wrote journalist and political researcher Frances Ryan. "They are battles to acknowledge that oppression doesn't come from a biological reality but a socially constructed inequality. They are concerned with idealised human bodies. They fight the structures and power that wish to control them; in sex, in work, in reproduction."[4] Like feminists against the patriarchy, disability activists work against an ableist society, or one that is prejudiced against

As with the patriarchy, in an ableist society, obstacles that are easily overcome by some are roadblocks to others.

people with disabilities. Women and people of other genders who have disabilities deal with ableism and sexism, both of which attempt to exert control over their bodies.

Ableism also plays into society's issues surrounding mental health, which is something many feminists are concerned with.

Traditionally, people with all kinds of mental health conditions or developmental disorders—including autism, depression, schizophrenia, attention-deficit/hyperactivity disorder (ADHD), and more—have been discriminated against and seen as scary, out of control, or broken in some way. In recent years, activists have worked to promote the idea of neurodivergence, a philosophy that says people's brains, like their bodies, are all different. While many mental illnesses and disorders can and often should be treated to improve the person's quality of life, the simple fact that they aren't neurotypical, or mentally "normal," is not something they should be ashamed of.

People who advocate for support of neurodivergent people work against the ideas that they are lazy, disorganized, disruptive, or dangerous just because they don't meet society's behavioral expectations. For example, some people with autism or ADHD are restless in class, causing them to move around or talk out of turn. Fidget spinners were designed in the 1990s to help them by giving them a way to release that nervous energy and make it easier for them to sit still and pay attention. However, in 2017, fidget spinners suddenly exploded in popularity and became the hot new toy. For neurotypical people, they were more distracting than helpful, leading some schools to ban them—thereby hurting the people they were invented for. Anti-ableist advocates want neurodivergent people to be seen as different, not wrong or bad, and want society to help them meet their needs in ways that might seem unusual, rather than forcing them to conform to a standard of behavior it's often hard for them to meet.

Socioeconomic Class

Economists define class as a category based on someone's economic position, meaning how much power and influence one has in the economy. This power and influence comes from how much money a person has. Generally, the most basic classes are upper, middle, working, and lower, although all of these except working class can be further divided in two. Each class has a certain amount of economic power. Upper-class people, such as CEOs of major corporations, make the most money and make up about

3 percent of the population in the United States. The upper-upper class, or the top 1 percent of the population, consists of billionaires, while the lower-upper class consists of millionaires. People in the middle class are generally highly educated and have professional jobs as doctors, lawyers, and businesspeople. They make up about 40 percent of the population and can be divided into upper-middle and lower-middle, depending on their income. The working class is made up of the 30 percent of the population that has a job but no college degree, which limits how much employers are generally willing to pay them. The lower class, which is made up of the working poor and the underclass, makes up 27 percent of the population. The working poor tend to have a high school degree or less and work in clerical or service positions. The underclass is likely to only be employed part-time or unemployed. Both categories of the lower class live either at or below the poverty line, and since they rarely have savings to fall back on, they're the ones who are most at risk of falling below the poverty line due to an unexpected illness or job loss.

Western culture uses a capitalist economic model, which means that trade and industry are owned by individuals rather than by the government. The main focus of capitalism is profit, or making money. In a capitalist society, economic class becomes socioeconomic class, meaning that one's economic power translates into how much power they have in society as a whole.

Feminists often criticize capitalism. Because it relies on lower-class workers to provide the labor that creates profit for the upper classes, many see it as a system built on inequality. In regard to women, writer

Erin McKelle commented, "When women have lower economic standing, they have less power and autonomy across all areas of their lives. Money, after all, is power."[5]

Patriarchy and capitalism often go hand in hand to perpetuate the oppression of women and other groups. Shown here are lower-class employees working in a lampshade factory under poor conditions in the 1920s. Because these employees were poor, black, and female, it was easy for their employer to take advantage of them.

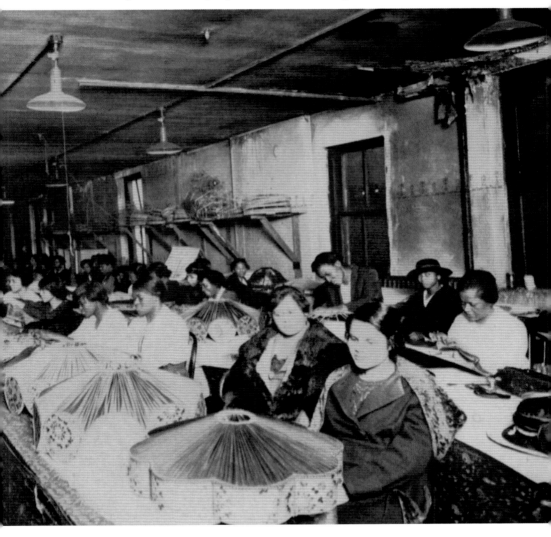

Many also believe that gender roles are a product of capitalism. In order to sell things in a free market and continue making a profit, companies have to make their products seem necessary. For example, makeup corporations subtly tell women that they need to change how their faces look in order to be socially acceptable, reinforcing unattainable, gendered standards for people's appearances. Other companies want to make it seem like every household needs two of everything—one for the women and one for the men—so it benefits them to enforce gender stereotypes.

Gender roles and capitalism tend to reinforce each other in ways that are harmful to both men and women. As professor Yen Lê Espiritu explained:

> *Because patriarchy mandates that men be the breadwinners, it pressures them to work in the capitalist wage market, even in jobs that are low paying, physically punishing, and without opportunities for upward mobility ... The assumption that women are not the main income earners in their families, and therefore can afford to work for less, provides ideological justification for employers to hire women at lower wages and in poorer working conditions than exist for men.*[6]

One issue within feminism is classism, or discrimination against a particular class—generally the lower classes. Many working- and lower-class women feel excluded by the feminist movement because "feminism has become increasingly academic, meaning you have to be educated to be taken seriously," pointed out teacher Tracy Powell. "Put that together and you'll get a lot of working-class females out there who feel they have no voice. Issues that may be important to feminism, like the politics of language, seem very abstract to working-class girls ... It's not real to them, the ideologies and analysis that are priceless to middle-class women aren't practical to them."[7] Activist Pavan Amara interviewed Powell and other working-class women from London, England, about their perspective on feminism. Another woman, Samantha Grover, responded, "You hear talk of working-class women, but of the feminist conferences and meetings I've attended I've never seen them get a teenage mum up on stage or talk about why female crime is rising, or anything outside of that white, middle-class [authority]."[8] Some activists are trying to find ways to include working- and lower-class women by creating less formal women's groups that focus on discussing experiences and allowing those experiences to inform feminist topics.

Checking Privilege

A privilege is a special right or advantage that's only available to a certain person or group. There are many layers of privilege that a person can have: Being a man is a privilege, but so is being white, cisgender, straight, upper-class, and able-bodied, and people's outlook on society is colored by the different privileges that they have.

As writer and Harvard Law School alumnus Brando Simeo Starkey pointed out in relation to race, "[White Americans] feel as if black folk, other minorities, immigrants and refugees have cut ahead of them in line, meaning the government caters to others before them. The line-cutting angers them, although they never question why they should occupy the first position."[9] This same mindset applies to any kind of privilege.

This doesn't mean that being white, straight, cis, or male is inherently bad. Having privilege doesn't automatically make someone blind to the struggles of others—in fact, many privileged people use their positions to make a difference and make sure less privileged people have their voices heard—and it also doesn't make someone immune to hardship. In a column for the *Chicago Tribune*, Dahleen Glanton wrote:

> *Being privileged does not necessarily mean that you have a perfect life. It does not mean that you come from wealth or that you always obtain everything you want—or deserve. It doesn't give you a pass to be lazy and shiftless. It doesn't automatically guarantee you success. White skin no more relieves you of taking responsibility for your life, working hard and thinking smart than it does for people with dark skin. It just means that you have a head start over the rest of us.*[10]

Some privileged people worry that when women and people of color receive certain advantages, they're "cutting in line." One example is that, when some state governments announced they would reduce or eliminate the "tampon tax," many men were angry that some products for men were still taxed—even though male products that are currently taxed aren't essential the way pads and tampons are.

Privileged people need to be willing to recognize their biases and change problematic behaviors—practices often collectively known as checking their privilege. Problems arise when people get defensive and burrow back into the safety that their position of power gives them.

Your Opinion Matters!

1. Why is intersectional feminism important?

2. Why do you think feminism has become an academic topic? Why does feminism often leave out working-class women?

3. Pick two topics from this chapter and explain how they could intersect with each other.

CHAPTER FIVE

THE FUTURE FEMINISTS WANT

Feminism's main goal is to achieve gender equality, but gaining equality is a process that will take many years. There are many issues to be tackled before sexism and misogyny disappear. However, feminists keep an ideal future in mind—one where everyone is truly equal regardless of who they are. Christina Jimenez, cofounder of the immigrant rights group United We Dream, said, "My vision is for a world and a country where people who have been kept on the margins, like immigrants and women and people of color, are able to live without fear and thrive."[1]

A Global Standard

Feminists are working toward creating a global standard of gender equality so people everywhere will be treated with respect. In 2015, the United Nations (UN) set 17 goals to meet by 2030, with the intention of improving the global community. The Global Goals for Sustainable Development include ending poverty and hunger, creating affordable clean energy, and ending inequality. On the web page for the fifth goal, gender equality, the UN noted, "Gender bias is undermining our social fabric and devalues all of us. It is not just a human rights issue; it is a tremendous waste of the

◀ The goal of feminism is to put everyone on an equal footing, making it easier for people to live well regardless of their sexual orientation, gender, race, class, ability, or any other factor.

The Women's March

On January 21, 2017, millions of people in the United States participated in the first Women's March on Washington, a protest centered on reproductive rights, civil rights, immigration, and many other social issues. The protest was in direct response to the inauguration of US president Donald Trump, who made sexist and racist comments throughout his presidential campaign that many felt made him unfit to lead the country. Speakers at the main demonstration in Washington, DC, included singer Janelle Monae, actress Scarlett Johansson, and feminist icon Gloria Steinem.

Although exact numbers are impossible to find, the *Washington Post* estimated that about 4 million people in the United States marched at 653 events across the country, making it likely to be the largest single-day protest in US history. Outside the United States, about 300,000 people marched in solidarity at 261 events. It was the first truly global protest—people demonstrated on every continent, including Antarctica, where about 30 tourists and scientists held signs with slogans such as "Seals for Science" and "Penguins for Peace." Although many people applauded the event, some pointed out that the leadership of the march displayed white feminism by excluding people of color in the organization phase. The following year, march organizers made an effort to be more intersectional, listening to and spotlighting people of color.

world's human potential. By denying women equal rights, we deny half the population a chance to live life at its fullest. Political, economic and social equality for women will benefit all the world's citizens."[2]

As of 2020, the United States still lags behind in terms of legal equality. In January 2020, 48 years after it was passed by Congress, the ERA was finally ratified in Virginia, the last state needed for the amendment to become law. Without the ERA, the US Constitution says nothing to protect women against

The Women's March focused on many feminist issues, such as sexual harassment and reproductive freedom.

discrimination. However, other states that previously ratified the amendment have since withdrawn their support. ERA supporters believe that even if the law needs to be rewritten and a new vote taken, the Constitution should still say something about equal rights among genders. Supreme Court justice Ruth Bader Ginsburg said of the amendment, "I would like my granddaughters, when they pick up the Constitution, to see that notion—that women and men are persons of equal stature—I'd like them to see that is a basic principle of our society."[3]

"Smash the Patriarchy"

Ending the patriarchy is an important part of gender equality. "Smash the patriarchy" is a common phrase feminists use when they talk about this. By nature, a social system that prioritizes one gender above all others is unequal, but there has never been a truly equal social system in any society in the history of the world. Going forward, feminists want to create a new kind of social system. However, although many people have ideas about what this new system will look like, no one can know for sure how it will end up being put into place. Many feminists hope that by continually making changes, the patriarchy can be replaced piece by piece. This is complicated, though, because so many different issues are intertwined that it can be difficult and overwhelming to know where to begin.

One issue that feminists believe could be key in changing the way society runs is the issue of childcare. In modern society, many women work, but they're still expected to be the primary caregiver for their children. Feminists believe this is unfair because men are generally not expected to care for their children above their careers and interests. To fix this problem, some have proposed a government-funded childcare system. Raina Lipsitz, a writer for the news website Al Jazeera America, discussed the benefits of such a system:

> Raising healthy, cared-for children would be a societal endeavor, not a personal problem. It would be possible for every American woman, not just a privileged few, to opt out of being her children's sole or primary caretaker and focus on her career, as men have always been able to do. It would be possible for thousands of women who dreamed of becoming doctors or engineers or bus drivers or starting businesses or running for office—only to be discouraged by the expectation that they spend their nonworking hours caring for children—to fulfill their professional ambitions ... They could make decisions about career, housing and relationships freely, not out of economic need.[4]

Making childcare more affordable and easily accessible would give many women more freedom.

Putting this kind of system in place doesn't mean that women wouldn't love and spend time with their children. It simply means they wouldn't have to give up their careers to do so. The current family model in Western society is a relatively new historical development. In the past, childcare was a collective effort, with extended family members and friends caring for the kids together. Some modern-day societies still operate this way.

A smaller step toward this goal would be removing the stigma, or negative view, against stay-at-home dads. Although it's becoming more common for fathers to stay home with their children while their partner works, it's still sometimes seen as a joke. Discarding this stigma would give parents more opportunities to structure their family lives as they see fit. Some people feel that the way Western society operates is the natural order of things and can't be changed, but other world cultures prove this view false. One example of a society that has successfully overcome the stigma attached to behaving outside gender roles is that of the Aka people in central Africa. There, men and women perform the same tasks without any stigma attached, and many Aka men care for their children while their wives go out and hunt.

Another goal feminists have in regard to children is making it socially acceptable for women not to have them at all. Today, women are expected to have children—often more than one— and to find joy and fulfillment in motherhood, constantly putting their children ahead of her own needs and wants. Women who don't do so tend to be shamed and labeled "bad mothers." In an article for the *Guardian*, journalist Stefanie Marsh wrote, "Social media has magnified this: taut, post-baby bodies on Instagram; mother-and-child selfies used as profile pictures on Facebook; motherhood has become an alternative identity rather than a rite of passage."[5] However, the role of motherhood isn't one every woman wants. While attitudes toward such women have improved a bit over time, many people still consider it horrifying and unnatural for a woman to either say she doesn't want children or to admit she regrets becoming a mother. Men are not viewed the same way and are more frequently portrayed in the media, such as on TV shows and in commercials, as having to be convinced to have children by their wife or being such incompetent caregivers that the mother can't trust him to be alone with the kids. This patriarchal standard also creates a stigma around men who prefer to stay home with their children.

Healthy Sexuality

To fight back against the patriarchy's control over people's bodies—and particularly over women's sexuality—feminists tend to support a sex-positive view of the future. Sex positivity is often defined as "the idea that all sex, as long as it is healthy and explicitly consensual, is a positive thing."[6] In a sex-positive future, people would not be shamed for being sexual or made to feel guilty for not being sexual. People's sexual lives would be their own business as long as no one was being abused and both partners enjoyed the experience. In the past, sex was seen as being more for the man, and it's only in recent years that women have spoken up about enjoying it as well instead of focusing only on the man's desires.

An important part of creating a sex-positive future is teaching the concept of consent. Consent is essentially permission, and feminists believe that everyone should ask for consent before doing anything to anyone, sexual or not. Getting consent is ultimately about respecting people's boundaries. For children, teaching consent is as easy as making sure they understand that no means no and that they're allowed to not want to hug or be hugged by someone, no matter who that someone is—even family members. As these kids grow into adults, these lessons will help shape them into people who know their boundaries and how to respect other people's boundaries, and feminists believe this will decrease the rates of physical and sexual violence, helping people live more safely and securely.

Awareness for Men

Although some feminists believe that change can be made without men, others believe that cis male support is necessary for feminism's success. Men, they say, should also be feminists.

"Men probably bear more of the responsibility for ending oppression of women since patriarchal men have been the main perpetrators of that very oppression,"[7] wrote Brian Klocke for the National Organization for Men Against Sexism (NOMAS). However, men also need to recognize that their power and privilege set them apart, so they should not expect to be welcomed into all feminist circles with open arms. Giving up some of that power so others can take the lead is one of the first steps to being pro-feminist.

An important part of feminism for cis men is supporting women in leadership roles.

"Not All Men"

In discussions about sexual harassment, the wage gap, or almost any other feminist issue, men often use the phrase "not all men" to defend themselves and their gender or to downplay the seriousness of feminist issues. "Not all men are rapists," they might say, or "Not all men make more money than women." However, these arguments tend to miss the point of the discussion. Firstly, few women who bring up these topics mean "all men" when they say "men" or "a man." They're typically talking about a specific man or group of men, and they're not attacking men in general. Even in more general conversations about men, feminist anger tends to be directed at the patriarchy and the social systems that certain men, such as rapists or workplace misogynists, represent.

Secondly, it's not constructive to say "not all men." For women, any man could be dangerous, either physically or verbally, and there is no way to know the difference between a "good" man and a "bad" man just by looking at him. In order to stay safe, women are taught to assume any strange man is a potential threat, so telling a woman that not all men are dangerous is meaningless. Women know not all men are out to harm them, but they take precautions to keep themselves safe in case the man they're interacting with turns out to be dangerous. Often, women are shamed for assuming a man is dangerous but also shamed if they get hurt. People victim-blame, asking why she didn't do more to keep herself safe.

However, writer Suzannah Weiss suggested that there is a place for "not all men" in feminism. "We can talk about, for example, how not all men were assigned male at birth," she wrote, "not all men are attracted to women, and not all men are innately aggressive, unemotional, or other things men are stereotyped to be. And we can even talk about how not all men are rapists—when it's serving a purpose like, say, pointing out that sexual violence is not natural or normal."[1]

1. Suzannah Weiss, "6 Reasons 'Not All Men' Misses The Point, Because It's Derailing Important Conversations," Bustle, July 9, 2016, www.bustle.com/articles/171595-6-reasons-not-all-men-misses-the-point-because-its-derailing-important-conversations.

Men also need to confront the ways sexism and misogyny harm them too. The patriarchal culture of toxic masculinity forces men into unnatural boxes the same way it does to everyone else. Men who are kind, nurturing, and emotionally available are still often looked down on even though these should be genderless traits. "Misogyny … is a way to manipulate, shame, and control people, marginalizing not just women, but men, too," writer Noah Berlatsky commented. "And that's why men should be feminists … Misogyny is a cage for everyone. When I call myself a male feminist, I'm not doing it because I think I'm going to save women. I'm doing it because I think it's important for men to acknowledge that as long as women aren't free, men won't be either."[8]

Feeling Safe

Because of rape culture, women generally grow up being told how not to be sexually assaulted: Don't wear short skirts or low-cut shirts. Don't go for a walk at night. Don't talk to strangers. By the time they reach adulthood, women are well aware of their status as targets for violence, and this culture of fear affects many decisions that women make. "A strange man comes up to me at night, with a dark car and tinted windows, as I walk alone in an isolated area, and asks for something—anything—to get me near or into his car," wrote Amanda Carneglia for the Georgia college newspaper the *Red & Black*. "The solution is to run. Always run. Get as far away from a possible predator and around more people as soon as possible."[9]

Being a feminist means advocating for people's right to feel safe. Although most women don't feel afraid all the time, they're taught that they have more to fear than men. Similarly, trans and nonbinary people may also feel unsafe being themselves, in public and at home, if they fear being bullied or harmed for going against people's expectations. Feminists hope to create a culture where people don't need to fear for their safety simply because of who they are.

For many women, simply walking to their car alone at night can feel dangerous. Most men have never felt this specific fear.

Freedom of Expression

Feminism comes down to the argument that everyone should be free to live and express themselves however they want. Women should be allowed to be CEOs or housewives. Men should be allowed to wear dresses or suits. People should be allowed to love whoever they want and express their gender however they want.

People should be encouraged to follow their passions, even if they go against traditional gender roles.

Because humans created the patriarchy and gender roles, feminists believe humans can also change them or get rid of them entirely. Shifting to a new social system will take time and dedication, and people may not see the changes on a cultural level for many years. In the future, though, people will have very different concepts of gender, and feminists are working to make sure that those concepts are based in equality.

Your Opinion Matters!

1. Do you think a feminist future is achievable?
2. How can men work to smash the patriarchy?
3. How does the patriarchy limit freedom of expression?

GETTING INVOLVED

The following are some suggestions for taking what you've just read and applying that information to your everyday life.

- Confront sexism when you see it happening.

- Call others out on sexist or misogynistic remarks.

- Treat everyone with respect regardless of their gender.

- Make an effort to include people of all genders in group events, such as school projects, parties, and lunch tables.

- Try to notice your privilege in everyday life, and do what you can to level the playing field for others who have less privilege.

- If you're a cis man, listen to what women and people of other genders have to say and make an effort to understand their points of view.

- Be critical of the media and how women and people of other genders are portrayed.

- Be mindful of intersectionality and how someone's background impacts their life. Understand that when people bring up how race, physical ability, economic status, and other factors affect them, it's not dividing feminism.

- Support and respect women in leadership positions.

- Believe victims of sexual assault, and avoid victim-blaming or slut-shaming them.

- Learn about consent, and practice setting boundaries on your personal space and respecting the boundaries of others.

- Ask your parents' permission to attend a protest about a cause that affects women or people of other genders. Research the cause beforehand to understand what you're protesting.

Introduction: What Is Feminism?

1. "Feminism," *Merriam-Webster*, accessed February 12, 2020, www.merriam-webster.com/dictionary/feminism.

2. Quoted in Sean Illing, "What We Get Wrong About Misogyny," Vox, modified February 7, 2018, www.vox.com/identities/2017/12/5/16705284/metoo-weinstein-misogyny-trump-sexism.

3. Quoted in Illing, "What We Get Wrong About Misogyny."

Chapter One: A Social Construct

1. Carol Bainbridge, "Why Social Constructs Are Created," VeryWell Family, modified September 12, 2019, www.verywellfamily.com/definition-of-social-construct-1448922.

2. David Rettew, "Nature Versus Nurture: Where We Are in 2017," *Psychology Today*, October 6, 2017, www.psychologytoday.com/us/blog/abcs-child-psychiatry/201710/nature-versus-nurture-where-we-are-in-2017.

3. "Gender and Genetics: Genetic Components of Sex and Gender," World Health Organization, accessed February 10, 2020, www.who.int/genomics/gender/en/index1.html.

4. Quoted in Elizabeth Weingarten, "How to Shake Up Gender Norms," *TIME*, January 20, 2015, time.com/3672297/future-gender-norms.

5. "Gender, Equity and Human Rights: Glossary of Terms and Tools," World Health Organization, accessed February 10, 2020, www.who.int/gender-equity-rights/knowledge/glossary/en.

6. Mari Mikkola, "Feminist Perspectives on Sex and Gender," Stanford Encyclopedia of Philosophy, modified October 25, 2017, plato.stanford.edu/entries/feminism-gender.

7. Quoted in "Can Gender-Specific Toys Affect a Child's Development? Researchers Weigh In," CBC Radio, modified December 18, 2017, www.cbc.ca/radio/thecurrent/the-current-for-december-18-2017-1.4451239/can-gender-specific-toys-affect-a-child-s-development-researchers-weigh-in-1.4451295.

8. Dina Gerdeman, "How Gender Stereotypes Kill a Woman's Self-Confidence," Harvard Business School, February 25, 2019, hbswk.hbs.edu/item/how-gender-stereotypes-less-than-br-greater-than-kill-a-woman-s-less-than-br-greater-than-self-confidence.

9. Quoted in Jeanne Maglaty, "When Did Girls Start Wearing Pink?," *Smithsonian*, April 7, 2011, www.smithsonianmag.com/arts-culture/when-did-girls-start-wearing-pink-1370097.

10. Michael Salter, "The Problem With a Fight Against Toxic Masculinity," *The Atlantic*, February 27, 2019, www.theatlantic.com/health/archive/2019/02/toxic-masculinity-history/583411.

11. Amanda Marcotte, "Overcompensation Nation: It's Time to Admit That Toxic Masculinity Drives Gun Violence," Salon, June 13, 2016, www.salon.com/2016/06/13/overcompensation_nation_its_time_to_admit_that_toxic_masculinity_drives_gun_violence.

Chapter Two: A History of Rebellion

1. "The Ascent of Woman: Is Gender Inequality Man-Made?," BBC Two, August 29, 2015, www.bbc.co.uk/programmes/articles/4vD023d-n4cp8wF2lRntcQ7L/is-gender-inequality-man-made.

2. Quoted in Mary R. Lefkowitz and Maureen B. Fant, *Women's Life in Greece and Rome: A Source Book in Translation* (London, UK: Bloomsbury Academic, 2016), p. 173.

3. Christine de Pisan, *The Book of the City of Ladies*, trans. Earl J. Richards. (New York, NY: Persea Books, 1998), p. 155.

4. John Ruskin, *Sesame and Lilies* (Chicago, IL: Scott, Foresman and Company, 1906), pp. 121–22.

5. "Declaration of Sentiments," National Park Service, modified February 26, 2015, www.nps.gov/wori/learn/historyculture/declaration-of-sentiments.htm.

6. Lori D. Ginzberg, interview by Steve Inskeep, "For Stanton, All Women Were Not Created Equal," NPR, July 13, 2011, www.npr.org/2011/07/13/137681070/for-stanton-all-women-were-not-created-equal.

7. Martha Rampton, "Four Waves of Feminism," Pacific University, October 25, 2015, www.pacificu.edu/about/media/four-waves-feminism.

8. Betty Friedan, "The National Organization for Women's 1966 Statement of Purpose," NOW, October 29, 1966, now.org/about/history/statement-of-purpose.

9. Rampton, "Four Waves of Feminism."

Chapter Three: Fourth-Wave Feminism

1. Natashya Gutierrez, "The Role of Social Media in Women Empowerment," Rappler, May 17, 2017, www.rappler.com/rappler-blogs/170047-social-media-feminism-women-empowerment.

2. Quoted in Angela Stringfellow, "Is the Gender Wage Gap a Myth or Reality? 27 Experts Debate the Wage Gap Issue," Wonolo, modified July 6, 2018, www.wonolo.com/blog/gender-wage-gap-myth-or-real/.

3. Quoted in Dina Gerdeman, "How Gender Stereotypes Kill a Woman's Self-Confidence," Harvard Business School, February 25, 2019, hbswk.hbs.edu/item/how-gender-stereotypes-less-than-br-greater-than-kill-a-woman-s-less-than-br-greater-than-self-confidence.

4. Henrik Kleven, Camille Landais, and Jakob Egholt Søgaard, "Children and Gender Inequality: Evidence from Denmark," National Bureau of Economic Research, January 2018, working paper no. 24219.

5. Leora Tanenbaum, "The Truth about Slut-Shaming," *HuffPost*, modified December 6, 2017, www.huffpost.com/entry/the-truth-about-slut-shaming_b_7054162.

6. Quoted in Zerlina Maxwell, "Rape Culture Is Real," *TIME*, March 27, 2014, time.com/40110/rape-culture-is-real.

7. "Induced Abortion Worldwide," Guttmacher Institute, March 2018, www.guttmacher.org/fact-sheet/induced-abortion-worldwide.

8. Mariah Blake, "Mad Men: Inside the Men's Rights Movement—and the Army of Misogynists and Trolls It Spawned," *Mother Jones*, January/February 2015, www.motherjones.com/politics/2015/01/warren-farrell-mens-rights-movement-feminism-misogyny-trolls.

9. Quoted in Lara Whyte, "'Young Men Should Be Furious': Inside the World's Largest Gathering of Men's Rights Activists," openDemocracy *50.50*, July 25, 2018, www.opendemocracy.net/5050/lara-whyte/young-men-should-be-furious-inside-worlds-largest-mens-rights-activism.

Chapter Four: Intersectional Equality

1. Quoted in "What Does Intersectional Feminism Actually Mean?," International Women's Development Agency, May 11, 2018, iwda.org.au/what-does-intersectional-feminism-actually-mean.

2. Julia Serano, "Trans Feminism: There's No Conundrum About It," *Ms.*, April 18, 2012, msmagazine.com/blog/2012/04/18/trans-feminism-theres-no-conundrum-about-it/.

3. Mari Mikkola, "Feminist Perspectives on Sex and Gender," Stanford Encyclopedia of Philosophy, modified October 25, 2017, plato.stanford.edu/entries/feminism-gender.

4. Frances Ryan, "'It's Not Only Steps That Keep Us Out': Mainstream Feminism Must Stop Ignoring Disabled Women," *New Statesman America*, May 20, 2014, www.newstatesman.com/society/2014/05/its-not-only-steps-keep-us-out-mainstream-feminism-must-stop-ignoring-disabled-women.

5. Erin McKelle, "7 Reasons Why Class Is a Feminist Issue," *Everyday Feminism*, September 1, 2014, everydayfeminism.com/2014/09/class-is-a-feminist-issue.

6. Yen Lê Espiritu, *Asian American Women and Men: Labor, Laws, and Love* (Walnut Creek, CA: AltaMira Press, 2000), p. 116.

7. Quoted in Pavan Amara, "Feminism: Still Excluding Working Class Women?," *The F-Word*, March 7, 2012, thefword.org.uk/2012/03/feminism_still_.

8. Quoted in Amara, "Feminism: Still Excluding Working Class Women?"

9. Brando Simeo Starkey, "Why Do so Many White People Deny the Existence of White Privilege?," *Undefeated*, March 1, 2017, theundefeated.com/features/why-do-so-many-white-people-deny-the-existence-of-white-privilege.

10. Dahleen Glanton, "Column: Yes, White 'Privilege' Is Still the Problem," *Chicago Tribune*, March 29, 2018, www.chicagotribune.com/news/columnists/glanton/ct-met-white-privilege-dahleen-glanton-20180328-story.html.

Chapter Five: The Future Feminists Want

1. Quoted in Emma Goldberg, "What's the Future of the Feminist Movement? 12 Leading Voices Respond," Vice, March 1, 2019, www.vice.com/en_us/article/zmayzx/future-of-feminism-roxane-gay-bell-hooks-longpath.

2. "Goal 5: Gender Equality," Global Goals, accessed February 10, 2020, next.globalgoals.org/5-gender-equality.

3. Quoted in Raina Lipsitz, "Imagine There's No Patriarchy," Al Jazeera America, December 31, 2014, america.aljazeera.com/opinions/2014/12/feminism-equal-rightsamendmentabortionbillcosby.html.

4. Lipsitz, "Imagine There's No Patriarchy."

5. Stefanie Marsh, "'It's the Breaking of a Taboo': The Parents Who Regret Having Children," Guardian, February 11, 2017, www.theguardian.com/lifeandstyle/2017/feb/11/breaking-taboo-parents-who-regret-having-children.

6. "Sex Positivity," Colorado State University Women and Gender Advocacy Center, accessed February 10, 2020, wgac.colostate.edu/education/the-body-is-political/sex-positivity.

7. Brian Klocke, "Roles of Men with Feminism and Feminist Theory," NOMAS, accessed March 4, 2019, nomas.org/roles-of-men-with-feminism-and-feminist-theory.

8. Noah Berlatsky, "Can Men Really Be Feminists?," The Atlantic, June 5, 2014, www.theatlantic.com/national/archive/2014/06/men-can-be-feminists-too/372234.

9. Amanda Carneglia, "Feminism Becomes a Necessity for Women's Safety," Red & Black, July 19, 2016, www.redandblack.com/opinion/feminism-becomes-a-necessity-for-women-s-safety/article_d2b57e20-4d17-11e6-bc3d-c74c86285f8d.html.

FOR MORE INFORMATION

Books: Nonfiction

Jensen, Kelly. *Here We Are: Feminism for the Real World*. Chapel Hill, NC: Algonquin Books, 2017.

Leon, Vicki. *4,000 Years of Uppity Women: Rebellious Belles, Daring Dames, and Headstrong Heroines Through the Ages*. New York, NY: MJF Books, 2011.

McCann, Hannah. *The Feminism Book*. New York, NY: DK Publishing, 2019.

Pitman, Gayle E. *Feminism from A to Z*. Washington, DC: Magination Press, 2017.

Rich, KaeLyn. *Girls Resist!: A Guide to Activism, Leadership, and Starting a Revolution*. Philadelphia, PA: Quirk Books, 2018.

Books: Fiction

Bourne, Holly. *What's a Girl Gotta Do?* London, UK: Usborne, 2016.

O'Neill, Louise. *Only Ever Yours*. New York, NY: Quercus, 2015.

Websites

Planned Parenthood

www.plannedparenthood.org

Planned Parenthood is a global health care provider that focuses on reproductive health and sex education. Its website provides information on birth control, pregnancy, STDs, and sexual orientation and gender.

National Organization for Men Against Sexism (NOMAS)

nomas.org

This organization focuses on men's issues within feminism, such as toxic masculinity and mental health. Visitors to its website will find resources on men's roles in eliminating racism, homophobia, gendered violence, and attacks on reproductive rights.

UltraViolet

weareultraviolet.org

UltraViolet is an organization that focuses on using political protests to win equal rights. Its website contains information about recent campaigns and how to get involved.

Women's Refugee Commission (WRC)

www.womensrefugeecommission.org

This organization works to protect the rights of women and children who have been displaced from their home countries. Its website provides information on global women's issues.

Organizations

American Civil Liberties Union (ACLU)
125 Broad Street, 18th Floor
New York, NY 10004
www.aclu.org
twitter.com/aclu
www.youtube.com/aclu
This nationwide organization fights to defend individuals' rights, including women and LGBTQ+ people. Through its network of activists and lawyers, the ACLU often goes to court to uphold the Bill of Rights.

Association for Women's Rights in Development (AWID)
215 Spadina Avenue, Suite 150
Toronto, ON M5T 2C7
Canada
www.awid.org
www.instagram.com/awidwomensrights/
twitter.com/AWID
www.youtube.com/user/AWIDNews
This organization works to influence government policies through advocacy and campaigning. It specializes in feminist and gender justice movements and fights for equality around the world.

National Organization for Women (NOW)
1100 H Street NW, Suite 300
Washington, DC 20005
now.org
twitter.com/NationalNOW
www.youtube.com/user/NOWvideos
NOW works with communities and organizations across the United States to campaign for equal rights. It focuses on grassroots activism to promote feminist ideas, end discrimination, and make cultural change.

Rape, Abuse, and Incest National Network (RAINN)
hotline: (800) 656-4673
www.rainn.org
www.instagram.com/rainn/
twitter.com/rainn
www.youtube.com/user/RAINN01
This anti-sexual violence organization operates the National Sexual Assault Hotline and works to help survivors. It also provides programs to prevent sexual violence and bring perpetrators to justice. A live chat option is also available on its website 24/7.

Sylvia Rivera Law Project (SRLP)
147 W 24th Street, 5th Floor
New York, NY 10011
srlp.org
www.instagram.com/sylviariveralawproject/
twitter.com/srlp
www.youtube.com/user/SylviaRiveraLP
This organization works to promote self-determination in gender identity and expression. It focuses on raising awareness of the racial, social, and economic injustices that prevent gender self-determination.

A

ableism, 61, 67–69
abortions, 39, 56–58
assault, 9, 20, 34, 49, 54–55, 59, 62, 86
assigned gender, 13, 16, 64
assigned sex, 13, 15–17, 64

B

Banet-Weiser, Sarah, 51
Berlatsky, Noah, 86
birth control pills, 8, 37
bodily autonomy, 56, 58
Boudicca, 28
Bow, Clara, 39
Burke, Tarana, 49
Butler, Judith, 14

C

capitalism, 70–72
careers, 6, 9, 16, 19, 37, 50, 52–54, 80, 82
Carneglia, Amanda, 86
Cavendish, Margaret, 31
celebrities, 43, 49–50
children, 6, 14–18, 20, 25–26, 37, 54, 59, 80, 82–83
chromosomes, 11–12, 15
classism, 43, 61, 72
clothing, 16–17, 20, 22, 63
Code of Hammurabi, 25
Coffman, Katherine B., 53
companies, 20, 22, 50–51, 72

consent, 83, 90
Cooper, Anna J., 61

D

Davis, Angela, 61
Declaration of Sentiments, 34
de Pisan, Christine, 29
Dinella, Lisa, 17
disability rights, 66–67
domestic abuse, 7, 20, 54
Dreger, Alice, 13
dysphoria, 15, 18

E

Egypt, 26–28
Elam, Paul, 59
Equal Rights Amendment (ERA), 39, 42, 78–79
Espiritu, Yen Lê, 72

F

Farrell, Warren, 58
female hysteria, 34
Feminine Mystique, The (Friedan), 37, 62
feminine traits, 7, 23, 64
first-wave feminism, 34–36, 62
flappers, 38–39
Fourier, Charles, 5
fourth-wave feminism, 47–48
Friedan, Betty, 37–38, 62–63
Friedman, Jaclyn, 56

PHOTO CREDITS

Cover Jacob Lund/Shutterstock.com; pp. 4, 40–41 Bettmann/ Bettmann/Getty Images; p. 6 Alena A/Shutterstock.com; p. 8 abd/Shutterstock.com; p. 10 from2015/E+/Getty Images; p. 14 Tara Moore/DigitalVision/Getty Images; p. 17 Barbara Neveu/ Shutterstock.com; p. 21 GL Archive/Alamy Stock Photo; p. 24 Art Media/Print Collector/Getty Images; p. 27 Universal History Archive/UIG/Getty Images; p. 30 Picturenow/Universal Images Group via Getty Images; p. 33 De Agostini/Getty Images; p. 39 Eugene Robert Richee/John Kobal Foundation/Getty Images; p. 44 Chelsea Guglielmino/Getty Images News/Getty Images; p. 46 Zhang Peng/LightRocket via Getty Images; p. 52 Creative Touch Imaging Ltd./NurPhoto via Getty Images; p. 55 Noriko Hayashi/ Bloomberg via Getty Images; p. 57 © Viviane Moos/Corbis/Corbis via Getty Images; p. 60 Darrin Klimek/Photodisc/Getty Images; p. 65 Mateusz Slodkowski/SOPA Images/LightRocket via Getty Images; p. 68 Tatiana Belova/Shutterstock.com; pp. 70–71 Everett Historical/Shutterstock.com; p. 74 zoranm/E+/Getty Images; p. 76 Rawpixel.com/Shutterstock.com; p. 79 Amru Salahuddien/ Anadolu Agency/Getty Images; pp. 80–81 Mark Wilson/Getty Images; p. 84 fizkes/Shutterstock.com; p. 87 LightField Studios/ Shutterstock.com; p. 88 kali9/E+/Getty Images.

ABOUT THE AUTHOR

Michelle Denton is a copy editor of young adult nonfiction as well as a freelance writer. She received her bachelor's degree in English and creative writing from Canisius College in 2016, graduating cum laude from the All-College Honors Program. She lives in Buffalo, New York, and enjoys annoying her cats and decorating in her spare time.